CIMA

Case Study

Management Level

Study Text

CIMA PUBLISHING

KAPLAN PUBLISHING

Published by: Kaplan Publishing UK

Unit 2 The Business Centre, Molly Millars Lane, Wokingham, Berkshire RG41 2QZ

Acknowledgements

We are grateful to the CIMA for permission to reproduce past examination questions. The answers to CIMA Exams have been prepared by Kaplan Publishing, except in the case of the CIMA November 2010 and subsequent CIMA Exam answers where the official CIMA answers have been reproduced.

Notice

British Library Cataloguing in Publication Data

A catalogue record for this book is available from the British Library.

ISBN: 978-1-78415-526-1

Printed and bound in Great Britain.

Contents

Paper Introduction

Acknowledgements

Every effort has been made to contact the holders of copyright material, but if any here have been inadvertently overlooked the publishers will be pleased to make the necessary arrangements at the first opportunity.

How to Use the Materials

Icon Explanations

Test Your Understanding – following key points and definitions are exercises which give the opportunity to assess the understanding of these core areas. Within the work book the answers to these sections are left blank, explanations to the questions can be found within the online version which can be hidden or shown on screen to enable repetition of activities.

Illustration – to help develop an understanding of topics and the test your understanding exercises the illustrative examples can be used.

Quality and accuracy are of the utmost importance to us so if you spot an error in any of our products, please send an email to mykaplanreporting@kaplan.com with full details, or follow the link to the feedback form in MyKaplan.

Our Quality Coordinator will work with our technical team to verify the error and take action to ensure it is corrected in future editions.

Exam Introduction

To complete the CIMA qualification and be able to use the designatory letters of ACMA and CGMA, candidates for this prestigious award need to achieve three things:

- attain the entry requirements for the professional level qualification

- study for and complete the relevant professional level assessments and examinations

- complete three years of relevant practical experience

This text concentrates on the second of these requirements, and in particular to study for and complete the management case study exam.

Overview of exam

The integrated case study exam will be available four times a year. The purpose of this exam is to consolidate learning at each level by reflecting real-life work situations. The exam is human marked.

This approach allows a wide range of knowledge and skills to be tested including research and analysis, presentation of information and communication skills whilst still ensuring competence in key skills.

CIMA believe that this new format will provide the commitment to delivering the competencies which employers desire thereby improving 'employability'.

For example, the management case study exam will be set within a simulated business context, placing the candidate in the job role matched to the competency level. In the case of the management level the job role is senior manager and the competency level is described as "Monitor" requiring the candidate to demonstrate the ability to monitor implementation of strategy and ensure corrective action is taken.

The exam is intended to replicate "a day in the life" of a finance professional operating at the management level and provide a simulated environment for candidates to demonstrate the required level of proficiency in each of the competency areas. Consequently, the exam will be set and marked according to the competency weightings at the level.

The integrated case study exam is 3 hours in duration and is made up of a series of timed tests. Candidates will be provided with access to pre-seen information approximately seven weeks before the real exam.

Assessment aims and strategy

The integrated Case Study examinations combine the knowledge and learning from across the three pillars of the syllabus set in a simulated business context relating to one or more fictional business organisations which are in turn based on a real business or industry.

The integrated case study is three hours long. The case study will include both pre-seen and un-seen material, the latter being made available during the examination. They will incorporate short written answers, emails, letters and any form of appropriate communication required within the tasks set.

The focus is on application, analysis and evaluation which are levels 3, 4 and 5 of the CIMA hierarchy of verbs (see below).

Simulated business issues in the integrated case studies provide candidates with the opportunity to demonstrate their familiarity with the context and interrelationships of the level's technical content. This reflects the cross functional abilities required in the workplace. Skills will include research, analysis, presentation of both financial and non-financial information and communication skills.

Feedback will be provided to candidates with their results. Exam sittings for the case studies will occur every three months. Candidates must have completed or be exempt from the three objective tests at a particular level before attempting the relevant integrated case study.

Learning outcomes

Each syllabus topic from the objective test subjects contains one or more lead learning outcomes, related component learning outcomes and indicative syllabus content. This provides a guide for the likely content of the case study exam.

Each lead learning outcome:

- defines the skill or ability that a well-prepared candidate should be able to exhibit in an examination

- is examinable and demonstrates the approach likely to be taken in examination questions

The lead learning outcomes are part of a hierarchy of learning objectives. The verbs used at the beginning of each learning outcome relate to a specific learning objective as illustrated in the detail below. You will not necessarily see these verbs reflected in the case study requirements but they indicate the depth of knowledge required for particular topics. Requirements in the case study may be presented as requests for reports, presentations, etc, as well as simple tasks. The case study exam will focus on Levels 3, 4 and 5.

Level 1

Learning objective – Knowledge (What you are expected to know)

- List – Make a list of
- State – Express, fully or clearly, the details/facts of
- Define – Give the exact meaning of

Level 2

Learning objective – Comprehension (What you are expected to understand)

- Describe – Communicate the key features of
- Distinguish – Highlight the differences between
- Explain – Make clear or intelligible/State the meaning or purpose of
- Identify – Recognise, establish or select after consideration
- Illustrate – Use an example to describe or explain something

Level 3

Learning objective – Application (How you are expected to apply your knowledge)

- Apply – Put to practical use
- Calculate – Ascertain or reckon mathematically
- Demonstrate – Prove with certainty or exhibit by practical means
- Prepare – Make or get ready for use
- Reconcile – Make or prove consistent/compatible
- Solve – Find an answer to
- Tabulate – Arrange in a table

Level 4

Learning objective – Analysis (How you are expected to analyse the detail of what you have learned)

- Analyse – Examine in detail the structure of
- Categorise – Place into a defined class or division
- Compare and contrast – Show the similarities and/or differences between
- Construct – Build up or compile
- Discuss – Examine in detail by argument
- Interpret – Translate into intelligible or familiar terms
- Prioritise – Place in order of priority or sequence for action
- Produce – Create or bring into existence

Level 5

Learning objective – Evaluation (How you are expected to use your learning to evaluate, make decisions or recommendations)

- Advise – Counsel, inform or notify
- Evaluate – Appraise or assess the value of
- Recommend – Propose a course of action

How to use the material

These Official CIMA learning materials brought to you by CIMA and Kaplan Publishing have been carefully designed to make your learning experience as easy as possible and give you the best chances of success in your Integrated Case Study Examinations.

This Study Text has been designed with the needs of home study and distance learning candidates in mind. However, the Study Text is also ideal for fully taught courses.

The aim of this textbook is to walk you through the stages to prepare for, and to answer, the requirements of the Case Study Examination.

Practical hints and realistic tips are given throughout the book making it easy for you to apply what you've learned in this text to your actual Case Study Exam.

Where sample solutions are provided, they must be viewed as just one interpretation of the case. One key aspect, which you must appreciate early in your studies, is that there is no single 'correct' solution.

Your own answer might reach different conclusions, and give greater emphasis to some issues and less emphasis to others, but score equally as well if it demonstrates the required skills.

If you work conscientiously through the official CIMA Study Text according to the guidelines above, as well as analysing the pre-seen information in full, you will be giving yourself an excellent chance of success in your examination. Good luck with your studies!

Planning

To begin with, formal planning is essential to get the best return from the time you spend studying. Estimate how much time in total you are going to need for each subject you are studying for the Case Study Examination. You may find it helpful to read "Pass First Time!" second edition by David R. Harris ISBN 978-1-85617-798-6.

This book will provide you with proven study techniques. Chapter by chapter it covers the building blocks of successful learning and examination techniques and shows you how to earn all the marks you deserve, and explains how to avoid the most common pitfalls.

With your study material before you, decide which chapters you are going to study in each week, which weeks you will devote to practising past exams, and which weeks you will spend becoming familiar with your case study pre-seen material.

Prepare a written schedule summarising the above and stick to it! Students are advised to refer to articles published regularly in CIMA's magazine (Financial Management), the student e-newsletter (Velocity) and on the CIMA website, to ensure they are up to date with relevant issues and topics.

Tips for effective studying

(1) Aim to find a quiet and undisturbed location for your study, and plan as far as possible to use the same period of time each day. Getting into a routine helps to avoid wasting time. Make sure that you have all the materials you need before you begin so as to minimise interruptions.

(2) Store all your materials in one place, so that you do not waste time searching for items around your accommodation. If you have to pack everything away after each study period, keep them in a box, or even a suitcase, which will not be disturbed until the next time.

(3) Limit distractions. To make the most effective use of your study periods you should be able to apply total concentration, so turn off all entertainment equipment, set your phones to message mode, and put up your 'do not disturb' sign.

(4) Your timetable will tell you which area to study. However, before diving in and becoming engrossed in the finer points, make sure you have an overall picture of all the areas that need to be covered by the end of that session. After an hour, allow yourself a short break and move away from your Study Text. With experience, you will learn to assess the pace you need to work at.

(5) Work carefully through each chapter, making notes as you go. When you have covered a suitable amount of material, vary the pattern by attempting a practice exercise. When you have finished your attempt, make notes of any mistakes you made, or any areas that you failed to cover or covered more briefly.

(6) Make notes as you study, and discover the techniques that work best for you. Your notes may be in the form of lists, bullet points, diagrams, summaries, 'mind maps', or the written word, but remember that you will need to refer back to them at a later date, so they must be intelligible. If you are on a taught course, make sure you highlight any issues you would like to follow up with your lecturer.

(7) Organise your notes. Make sure that all your notes, calculations etc can be effectively filed and easily retrieved later.

(8) Attempt practice exercises and write out full answers. Reviewing these and reflecting on suggested solutions is a crucial part of your studies.

Relevant practical experience

In order to become a Chartered Global Management Accountant (ACMA, CGMA), you need a minimum of three years' verified relevant work-based practical experience.

Read the 'Applying for Membership' brochure for full details of the practical experience requirements (PER). At the time of print CIMA were in the process of updating these requirements for 2015.

Introduction to case study exams

Chapter learning objectives

- To gain an overview of the case study exam, its purpose, structure, marking and process involved.

1 Why a Case Study Examination?

The Case Study Examination is an attempt to simulate workplace problem solving, and allows examiners to move one step closer to the assessment of competence than is possible with objective test questions. It is a test of your professional competence.

CIMA wishes to assess:

- your possession of skills such as research, synthesis, analysis and evaluation, in addition to;
- your technical knowledge, and
- your skill in presenting and communicating information to users.

Since the examination tests a range of different skills, preparing for this examination needs to be different from studying for a 'traditional' examination. The purpose of this text is to suggest how you might prepare for the examination by developing and practising your skills.

2 Your role

Each case study exam will be set within a simulated business context, placing the candidate in the job role matched to the competency level.

In the case of the management level the job role is a manager reporting to the CFO and other senior managers within the organisation.

The competency level is described as "Monitor" requiring the candidate to demonstrate the ability to monitor implementation of strategy and ensure corrective action is taken.

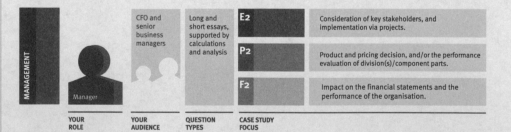

3 CIMA's Competency Framework

CIMA has developed a competency framework which explains the skills which a finance professional needs to possess in order to drive their organisation forward. This framework highlights the importance of not just accounting techniques but also wider business management skills. It also emphasises the need for complete integration of these many and varied skills. It is no longer sufficient for a finance professional to only display relevant technical ability.

The technical competencies are still important but in addition the accountant must have a good understanding of the organisation, it's environment and other relevant commercial knowledge. It is also important to possess the relevant people and leadership skills to ensure that technical and business knowledge is applied appropriately and effectively throughout the organisation.

The four generic competencies can be summarised as:

(1) Technical skills ('Do accounting and finance work')

(2) Business skills ('in the context of the business')

(3) People skills ('to influence people')

(4) Leadership skills ('and lead within the organisation')

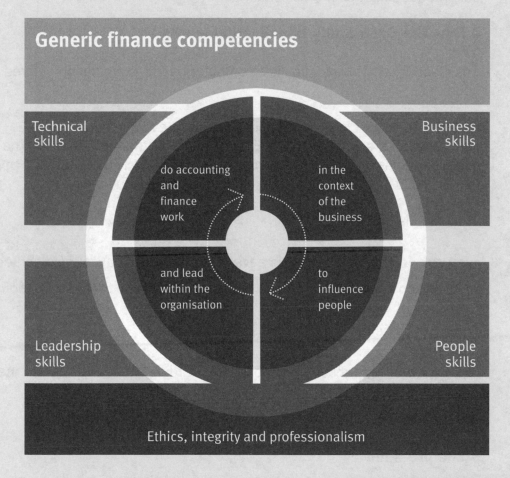

Generic finance competencies

Technical skills

Business skills

do accounting and finance work

in the context of the business

and lead within the organisation

to influence people

Leadership skills

People skills

Ethics, integrity and professionalism

CIMA recognise that the relevance of each of these competence areas will depend on the level a professional has progressed to within the organisation.

So for an entry level role (broadly equivalent to operational level), the core accounting and finance skills will form a large part of the role and only a small amount of leadership skill will be expected. This is reflected in the syllabus weightings. As you progress to management level it is anticipated that your role is more in line with a manager and therefore you will be expected to display a greater understanding of the business context and have developed more people and leadership skills.

At the strategic level the weightings for each of the four areas of competency are equal, reflecting the fact that as a senior manager you need to balance a broad range of skills.

Whilst the objective tests will examine your knowledge and ability to apply the underlying technical, business, people and leadership skills, the case study exam aims to test your ability to demonstrate and integrate these skills as a rounded finance professional.

4 How the Case Study Examination works

The Case Study Examination is a computer based examination of three hours.

Candidates cannot take the examination until they have successfully completed all the Objective Test Examinations for the relevant level. The exam comprises a series of requirements which aim to integrate and apply the technical knowledge tested in the Objective Test Examinations.

The exam is based on:

- pre-seen material issued in advance of the exam day, supplemented by

- additional, previously unseen material given to you in the exam room.

There will be several requirements, comprising:

(a) Triggers – information and updates regarding situations in which the company finds itself

(b) Tasks – work you will need to carry out based on the trigger

5 The pre-seen

CIMA releases the pre-seen material approximately seven weeks before the examination. This is posted on the student area of the CIMA website (www.cimaglobal.com) and it is your responsibility to download it.

The pre-seen material is an introductory scenario to set the scene for the case study, together with accounting and financial information. Much of the financial information will probably be in the form of appendices to the main text, but the main text of the pre-seen might include some figures too.

The pre-seen material is an extended scenario consisting of approximately 10 exhibits giving information about a business organisation. You will be taking on the role of a Finance Manager who works for the organisation, and your responses to the tasks will usually be addressed to your superior.

The pre-seen information for the Management level pilot exam (which concerns an airline) comprises:

An introduction to the company, market and economics of the industry

- Costing information
- Fleet information
- Share price information
- Summary of company directors
- Risk assessment
- Corporate social responsibility information
- Financial statement extracts
- Financial statement extracts for another airline

As you can see there is information relevant to all three management level technical subjects as well as information relevant to earlier papers.

The purpose of giving you access to this information in advance of the exam is to enable you to prepare notes, analyse and become very familiar with the organisation(s) and industry described. Remember, you have the role of a Finance Manager within this organisation and so you should use the pre-seen material to get a similar background knowledge as would be expected from someone in this situation.

Suggested approach to analysing the pre-seen information

(1) Detailed exhibit by exhibit analysis

As you review each exhibit ask yourself questions about what each piece of information means and what the implications of it might be for the organisation. Try to consider why the examiner might have provided this information.

(2) Technical analysis

Now it's time to apply many of the techniques you studied for the Objective Test Examinations to help you understand the organisation and the industry in which it operates in more depth. Some suggestions of what you could perform:

- Ratio analysis of financial statements and financial plans.

- Business strategy analysis, including generation of strategic options.
- Management accounting analysis, including costing, pricing and performance measurement.

It is important to bear in mind that this analysis will aid your understanding of the case study but you should not be determined to include the analysis in your responses unless clearly relevant to the requirement.

(3) Researching the industry involved

To ensure you have a good understanding of the context of the case, you could carry out some wider reading including researching the industry in which the organisation operates. For example, you could look at some of the real life key players and see what strategies they are adopting. Also consider key trends within the industry and the risks that have to be addressed. Finally you could consider what impact the economic climate or broader business influences (such as the political or regulatory environments) may be having on the industry.

You should not aim to spend too much time on this research as the pre-seen should be sufficient for your understanding of the industry. However a general appreciation of the 'real-world' should help to ensure you give sensible, commercial responses.

(4) Overall position analysis

Once you have completed all of the above, you should be able to stand back and see the bigger picture of the organisation within the case material. You should complete a position audit, including a SWOT analysis so you have a clear understanding of where the organisation is and where it might want to go.

(5) Identification of key issues

Using your SWOT analysis, you should now be able to identify a short list of key issues facing the organisation. An appreciation of these will assist you when understanding the issues introduced in the unseen material in the exam.

6 The unseen

In the examination you will be provided with:

- an on-screen version of the pre-seen material
- additional unseen information
- the requirements, broken down into a series of 4–6 tasks
- an on-screen calculator
- space to complete your answers

The unseen material will be a continuation of the pre-seen and will usually bring the scenario up to date. The unseen may focus on a number of issues that appeared in the pre-seen or it may just focus on one or two; either way it will provide the basis for the content of your answers.

A common mistake made by weaker students is that they place too much emphasis on their analysis of the pre-seen material and do not develop the information in the unseen material adequately. The key points to be referred to in your answer should be driven by the new information and specific tasks in the unseen material.

7 Triggers

Each requirement in the unseen material will begin with a **trigger**.

This will be information provided as an introduction to the work that you are required to complete.

The information may be in the form of a briefing by your superior, a newspaper article, some financial information or extracts from internal reports. You will be expected to integrate this new information with the analysis you have performed on the pre-seen material to produce a coherent and well informed response.

Here is an example of a trigger from the pilot exam:

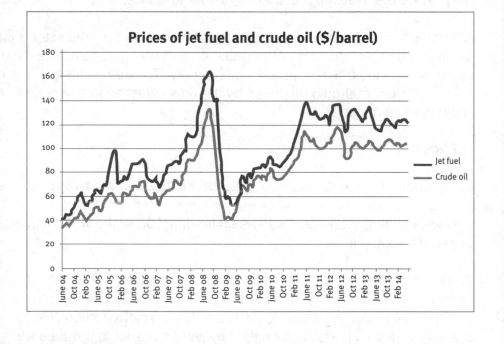

Example trigger from pilot exam

Today's newspapers are headlining with news of a significant increase in aviation fuel prices.

Air Fares Set To Rise As Jet Fuel Prices Soar

Unrest in the Middle East pushes crude oil prices to their highest level since 2008 this week. The airline industry seems set to be the biggest casualty of this increase because rising crude oil prices mean a corresponding hike in the cost of aviation fuel.

It is not yet clear whether the airlines will increase ticket prices in response to this development or whether they will attempt to absorb the increase in the hope that fuel prices return to their earlier level.

8 Tasks

Each section in the examination will take the form of a task you have been asked to complete, usually by your superior. These tasks can take various different forms, the most common are likely to be reports and email responses.

There is a time limit attached to each task and an onscreen timer will show you the time remaining for the task you are working on. Once you have submitted a task (or the time limit is reached, whichever is sooner) **you will not be able to return to that task**. If you still have time remaining you will be prompted to confirm you wish to move on to the next task before the previous task is completed and locked. This should reduce the problem of not completing the paper but does mean you will need to be very disciplined when attempting each task.

The Management level pilot exam comprises the following requirements:

- A report covering the increase in fuel prices as well as activity based and target costing

- A report concerning change management

- An email giving advice on negotiating with trade unions and planning for strike action

- A report covering integration of the company with a newly acquired subsidiary, issues in determining asset fair values and transfer pricing issues

Here is an example of a task from the pilot exam:

Example task from pilot exam

The Finance Director has sent you an email asking you to be part of a working party:

From: Michael Gibbons, Finance Director

Sent: 13th Feb, 10.21am

Subject: Re Working Party

I am setting up a working party that has been established to consider potential ways to reduce costs and increase revenues.

I am concerned that the scenario in which the price of aviation fuel is inflated may continue into the long term.

I would like us to suggest ways in which improved accounting might help the company to manage this problem.

Before the first meeting I would like you to prepare a report that covers two issues:

- Firstly, include a strategic analysis of the implications for Flyjet of a prolonged increase in fuel prices

- Secondly, include an evaluation of the ways in which the adoption of activity based management and target costing could be used to help us identify potential cost reduction opportunities.

Michael Gibbons

Finance Director
Flyjet
E: mg@Fly-jet.co.uk
T: 0161 233 3434

Prepare a report as detailed in the Finance Director's email.

9 Marking the Case Study

The Case Study Exams will be marked against the competencies summarised in section 2 of this chapter.

For the management level the weightings applied to these competencies are shown in the following diagram:

MANAGEMENT LEVEL

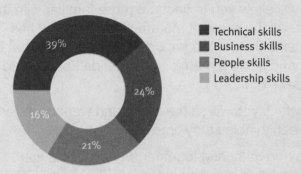

- ■ Technical skills
- ■ Business skills
- ■ People skills
- ■ Leadership skills

As you can see there is significantly less focus on your core accounting and finance skills as compared to the Operational Case Study and a greater focus on developing your people and leadership skills. This reflects the syllabus content for the exams within the Management level.

The following two chapters will explain further how these competencies relate to each syllabus and will also show the importance of integrating your knowledge of the three technical papers where possible and appropriate. You can also see in Chapter 11 how the competencies are applied in the marking of the pilot paper.

9.1 What you need to do to pass overall

There are two criterion that must be met to pass overall.

The overall mark is a "scaled" score based on the maximum marks available.

(1) Students must score over 60% overall.

(2) Students must score at least 33% of the marks available for each competency.

However, it is important to note that CIMA have advised students to focus on answering the requirements set rather than worrying about picking up marks for each competency. Marking guides are designed so that, if you answer the requirements set, then you will achieve the level of individual competency marks needed

10 Summary

You should now have a basic understanding of how the case study works. All of the ideas presented in this chapter will be explored further in the remainder of this textbook.

Next steps:

(1) It is a good idea to register with Pearson Vue to see the online version of the Pilot exam as this will allow you to become more familiar with the look and feel of the exam. All the relevant material from the Pilot has been reproduced in this textbook but it is important to recognise that the CIMA case study examinations are dynamic and shouldn't be viewed as equivalent to a static paper exam.

(2) Think about the date on which you will sit the exam and work backwards to create a sensible and achievable study timetable.

(3) It might be worth locating and gathering together any materials you already have from the supporting technical papers (E2, P2 and F2). We will show you in later chapters how you may need to use these materials.

Understanding competencies

Chapter learning objectives

- To understand how the learning outcomes from individual papers can be interpreted in terms of the competencies required for the case study exam.

1 Relevance of the Management level syllabus

Let us start by recapping the learning outcomes covered in the three individual management level papers.

E2 – Project and relationship management

Syllabus area A: INTRODUCTION TO STRATEGIC MANAGEMENT AND ASSESSING THE GLOBAL ENVIRONMENT (30%)

You must be able to explain	CIMA Official Study Text Chapter
<ul><li>What is 'strategy'</li><li>Strategic management</li><li>Levels of strategy</li><li>Rational approach including mission, SWOT and stakeholder analysis</li></ul>	Chapter 1 – The concept of strategy and the rational approach to strategy development
<ul><li>Pros/cons of rational approach</li><li>Uncertainty</li><li>Emergent approaches to strategy development</li><li>Incremental approaches to strategy development</li><li>Political approaches to strategy development</li><li>Strategy formulation in different contexts (SME, public sector, not-for-profit organisations)</li><li>The link between strategy and structure</li></ul>	Chapter 2 – Alternative approaches to strategy development
<ul><li>Competitive advantage</li><li>Generic competitive strategies</li><li>Resource based view</li><li>Resources/Value chain</li><li>Positioning approach</li><li>Sustainable competitive advantage</li></ul>	Chapter 3 – Competitive advantage

• Macro and micro environment • Globalisation • Country and political risk factors • Emerging markets • Porter's Diamond model • Porter's Five Forces model	Chapter 4 – Competitive environment
• Competitive analysis – role and key features • Collecting competitor information • Sources, types and quality of competitor information • Analysing and interpreting competitor data • Big Data	Chapter 5 – Competitive analysis

Syllabus area B: THE HUMAN ASPECTS OF THE ORGANISATION (20%)

You must be able to explain	CIMA Official Study Text Chapter
• Management concepts • Power/authority/delegation • Leadership approaches • Leadership in different contexts	Chapter 6 – Leadership and management
• HR policies and procedures • Equality and diversity • Discipline and grievance/dismissal and redundancy • Health and safety	Chapter 7 – HRM approaches to controlling performance
• Performance appraisals • Coaching and mentoring • Behavioural aspects of control • Performance measurement – target setting/MBO/Balanced Scorecard • Trust and control	Chapter 8 – Behavioural aspects of control

• Concept/importance • Levels • Influences – e.g. McKinsey 7S model • Cultural web • Models of culture – e.g. Handy • Hofstede	Chapter 9 – Organisational culture

Syllabus area C: MANAGING RELATIONSHIPS (20%)

You must be able to explain	CIMA Official Study Text Chapter
• Building teams • Leading and managing teams • Effective team work • Motivating team members • Resolving conflict in teams • Distributive leadership	Chapter 10 – Building, leading and managing teams
• Communication process/types/tools/problems • Importance of communication skills for Chartered Management Accountants (CMA) • Non-verbal communication and feedback • Influence/persuasion/negotiation • Sources and causes of conflict in organisations • Forms and types of conflict • Managing conflict	Chapter 11 – Techniques for managing organisational relationships
• Managing internal relationships with Finance • CMA as business partner • Shared service centres (SSC) and business process outsourcing (BPO) – with Transaction cost theory (contractual relationships/SLAs and co-creation) • Finance relationship with professional advisers	Chapter 12 – The Finance function and managing its relationships

Syllabus area D: MANAGING CHANGE THROUGH PROJECTS (30%)

You must be able to explain	CIMA Official Study Text Chapter
• Types of change • Triggers for change • Staged model of change management • Principles of change management • Problem identification as a precursor to change • Resistance to change • Managing resistance to change	Chapter 13 – Managing organisational change
• Definition of project attributes • Time, cost and quality objectives • Purpose/activities at key stages of project lifecycle • Role of project management (PM) methodologies	Chapter 14 – Managing projects
• PM tools (WBS, Gantt charts, networks, PERT, Scenario planning and buffering) • Managing project risk • PM software	Chapter 15 – Project management tools and techniques
• Project structures/matrix structure – impact on project achievement • Role and attributes of project manager • Role of CMA in projects • Role of other key players in projects • Managing key project stakeholders • Lifecycle of project teams • Leading and motivating project teams	Chapter 16 – People and projects

P2 – Advanced Management Accounting

Syllabus area A: COST PLANNING AND ANALYSIS FOR COMPETITIVE ADVANTAGE (25%)

You must be able to explain	CIMA Official Study Text Chapter
• Discuss the advantages and disadvantages of Activity Based Costing and Activity Based Management • Explain the benefits and limitations of ABC and its advanced applications such as DPP or CPA • Discuss the advantages and disadvantages of Activity Based Budgeting • Identify a Pareto situation	Chapter 1
• Explain why quality is becoming more important to industries • Explain TQM, JIT, Kaizen approaches, their pre-requisites, advantages and disadvantages • Explain the Business Process Re-engineering approach	Chapter 2
• Explain how a move away from traditional costing techniques can improve profitability • Explain target costing and cost reduction techniques • Apply the Value Chain model to business analysis • Explain throughput accounting	Chapter 3
• Apply learning curves principles to estimate time and cost for activities	Chapter 4

Syllabus area B: CONTROL AND PERFORMANCE MANAGEMENT OF RESPONSIBILITY CENTRES (30%)

You must be able to explain	CIMA Official Study Text Chapter
• Discuss the importance of responsibility accounting and the information needed by managers for decision making • Prepare reports to inform decisions • Recognise behavioural issues linked to the budgeting process and different degrees of participation • Discuss the pros and cons of the 'Beyond Budgeting' approach	Chapter 5
• Interpret key financial metrics of divisional performance, such as profitability, liquidity, asset turnover, return on investment, RI and EVA	Chapter 6
• Discuss issues arising from the use of performance measures and budgets for control • Discuss traditional and non traditional approaches to performance measurement • Manipulate non-financial performance indicators	Chapter 7
• Discuss transfer pricing systems • Explain the issues surrounding transfer pricing internationally, when different tax rates are involved	Chapter 8

Syllabus area C: LONG TERM DECISION MAKING (30%)

You must be able to explain	CIMA Official Study Text Chapter
• Identify the relevant cash flows for use in long-term decision making on investments • Identify non-financial factors in long-term decisions • Explain the different phases in the process of investment decision making, from origination of proposals to final decision • Explain the concept of the time value of money • Explain different techniques for Investment Appraisal	Chapters 9 and 10
• Explain price elasticity concepts • Discuss different pricing strategies, and their consequences • Explain different types of market structures in which a business operates, and the pricing implications of that business environment	Chapter 11

Syllabus area D: MANAGEMENT CONTROL AND RISK (15%)

You must be able to explain	CIMA Official Study Text Chapter
• Analyse risk and uncertainty; explain the difference between the two	Chapter 12
• Explain the difference between upside risk and downside risk • Apply the TARA framework to risk management • Discuss the ethical implications of decisions	Chapter 13
• Discuss the risk associated with the collection and use of information	Chapter 14

F2 – Advanced Financial Reporting

Syllabus area A: SOURCES OF LONG TERM FINANCE (15%)

You must be able to explain	CIMA Official Study Text Chapter
• Discuss the characteristics of different types of long-term debt and equity finance • Discuss the markets for and methods of raising long-term finance	Chapter 1 – Long term finance
• Calculate the cost of equity for an incorporated entity using the dividend valuation model • Calculate the post-tax cost of debt for an incorporated entity • Calculate weighted average cost of capital (WACC) for an incorporated entity	Chapter 2 – Cost of capital

Syllabus area B: FINANCIAL REPORTING (60%)

You must be able to:	CIMA Official Study Text Chapter
Produce primary financial statements for a group of entities in accordance with relevant international accounting standards. Primary financial statements in the syllabus are: • Consolidated statement of comprehensive income (profit or loss and other comprehensive income) • Consolidated statement of financial position	Chapter 12 – Basic group accounts – F1 syllabus
• Consolidated statement of changes in equity	Chapter 16 – Consolidated statement of changes in equity
• Consolidated statement of cash flows	Chapter 17 – Consolidated statement of cash flows
• IFRS 3 Business combinations (governs recognition and measurement of goodwill) • IFRS 11 Joint arrangements	Chapter 13 – Basic group accounts – F2 syllabus

Relevant accounting standards are: • IAS 1 Presentation of FS • IAS 27 Consolidated and separate FS • IAS 28 Investments in associates and JVs • IFRS 10 Consolidated FS (definition of control) • IFRS 3 Business combinations (governs recognition and measurement of goodwill) • IFRS 11 Joint arrangements	Chapter 12 Basic group accounts – F1 syllabus Chapter 13 – Basic group accounts – F2 syllabus
Discuss the need for and the nature of disclosures of interests in other entities (IFRS 12)	Chapter 13 – Basic group accounts – F2 syllabus
Discuss the provisions of relevant international accounting standards, and produce the accounting entries, in respect of the recognition and measurement of: • Revenue (IAS 18)	Chapter 7 Revenue and substance
• Leases (IAS 17)	Chapter 6 Leases
• Financial Instruments (IAS 32 & 39)	Chapter 3 Financial instruments
• Provisions (IAS 37)	Chapter 8 Provisions, contingent liabilities and contingent assets
• Share-based payments (IFRS 2)	Chapter 4 Share-based payments
• Deferred taxation (IAS 12)	Chapter 9 Deferred tax
• Construction contracts (IAS 11)	Chapter 10 Construction contracts
Discuss the ethical selection and adoption of relevant accounting policies and accounting estimates.	Chapter 3 to 10
Demonstrate impact of: • Acquiring additional shareholdings • Disposing of all or part of a shareholding	Chapter 15 Changes in group structure

Demonstrate impact of consolidating a foreign subsidiary	Chapter 18 Foreign currency translation
Demonstrate impact of acquiring indirect control of a subsidiary	Chapter 14 Complex groups
Discuss the need for and nature of disclosure of transactions between related parties	Chapter 11 Related parties
Calculate basic and diluted earnings per share (IAS 33)	Chapter 5 Earnings per share

Syllabus area C: ANALYSIS OF FINANCIAL PERFORMANCE AND POSITION (15%)

You must be able to explain	CIMA Official Study Text Chapter
• Calculate ratios relevant for the assessment of an entity's profitability, financial performance, financial position and financial adaptability.	Chapter 19 – Analysis of financial performance and position
• Evaluate the financial performance, financial position and financial adaptability of an entity based on the information contained in the financial statements provided.	Chapter 19 – Analysis of financial performance and position
• Advise on action that could be taken to improve an entity's financial performance and financial position	Chapter 19 – Analysis of financial performance and position
Discuss the limitations that can be caused by internal and external factors: • Inter-segment comparisons • International comparisons	Chapter 19 – Analysis of financial performance and position

2 Introduction to management level case study competencies

For the case study exam the individual paper learning outcomes are replaced/augmented/supplemented by four generic competencies.

As we explained in Chapter 1, at this level you will be tested on those competencies expected of a manager.

The weightings for the generic competencies are:

- Technical skills – 39%

- Business skills – 24%

- People skills – 21%

- Leadership skills – 16%

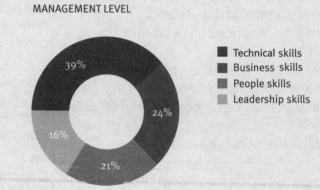

MANAGEMENT LEVEL

So you will be expected to show technical skills such as cost accounting from your P2 paper ('doing accounting and finance work') whilst taking into account the business context such as your understanding of the market environment from E2 ('in the context of the business'). You may then need to make decisions and communicate them using techniques learnt in P2 and E2 ('to influence people') and potentially advise on managing the resulting change process using skills learnt in E2 ('whilst leading within the organisation').

You should aim to be comfortable with the whole syllabus for all three subjects and should be ready to attempt the whole paper as there is a limit to the extent to which strength in one topic can compensate for weakness in another.

Let's examine each generic competency in more detail before thinking about integrating these skills. Remember a competency focuses on what you can DO rather than what you KNOW and so you need to think about this in terms of ability rather than simply knowledge.

3 The competencies in more detail

The generic competences and individual paper learning outcomes can be correlated as follows:

CIMA COMPETENCY FRAMEWORK			
Competencies	Syllabus area		
Technical skills	E2	P2	F2
Financial accounting and reporting			F2
Cost accounting and management		P2	
Planning and control		P2	
Management reporting and analysis		P2	
Corporate finance and treasury management			
Risk management and internal control		P2	
Taxation		P2	F2
Accounting information systems		P2	F2
Business skills			
Strategy	E2		
Market environment	E2		
Process management		P2	
Business relations	E2		
Project management	E2	P2	
Regulatory environment			F2
Macro-economic anlaysis	E2		
People skills			
Influence	E2		
Negotiation	E2		
Decision making	E2	P2	
Communication	E2		
Collaboration and partnering	E2		
Leadership skills			
Team building	E2		
Coaching and mentoring	E2		
Driving performance		P2	
Motivating and inspiring	E2		
Change management	E2		
Underpinned by ethics, integrity and professionalism			

This can be discussed in further detail as follows:

3.1 Technical skills

At the management level these skills will be drawn from the syllabus for papers E2, F2 and P2. Here is a sample of some of the competencies which you may be expected to demonstrate.

Note: this list should not be taken as exhaustive but is presented here to give you more of an idea how the case study works:

- I can interpret a Weighted Average Cost of Capital calculation
- I can advise on different methods for raising long term finance

---

e.g | **Illustration – 1**

Scenario/Trigger

X company has decided to purchase and redevelop a new factory. Finance is required.

Task

Discuss the pros and cons of using debt finance over raising further equity.

Suggested Approach

- Make a note of as many advantages and disadvantages of debt finance as you can

- Look for clues in the pre seen and unseen such as availability of assets on which to secure debt, current gearing levels, and who the current shareholders are.

- Discuss the pros and cons MOST RELEVANT to the company situation bringing in information from the pre seen and unseen where possible

---

- I can understand and interpret consolidated financial statements
- I can explain and apply relevant international accounting standards

e.g

Illustration – 2

Scenario/Trigger

G company is considering acquiring some plant and machinery through the use of a lease. The company is considering a five year lease for a machine with a useful economic life of five years. The company will be responsible for all associated costs of the machine including maintenance and insurance.

Task

Discuss the impact this machine is likely to have on the financial statements of G.

Suggested Approach

- Decide what the possible options are i.e finance lease of operating lease

- Consider what indications of a finance lease are indicated in the pre seen and unseen – don't just list all you know

- Conclude as to correct classification

- Consider impact on Statement of Financial Position (asset and liability) and income statement (depreciation)

- I can perform analysis on a set of financial statements and provide meaningful commentary

- I can advise on different methods of analysing and managing costs

Illustration – 3

Scenario/Trigger

F company manufactures cars. It has recently lost market share due to both pricing and quality issues so is considering modernising some of its operations.

Task

Explain the implications of implementing a Just-In-Time system of purchasing and production.

Suggested Approach

- Consider purchasing and production separately
- Make a note of all of the possible implications of JIT
- Decide which are particularly relevant for a car manufacturer

- I can prepare performance reports and discuss issues regarding performance measurement
- I can discuss divisionalisation and advise on a range of different transfer pricing systems

e.g

Illustration – 4

Scenario/Trigger

C company has recently acquired one of its main component suppliers. Disagreements have since arisen over transfer pricing within the group.

Task

Evaluate the available transfer pricing systems and make a recommendation.

Suggested Approach

- Make a note of the main systems you know with a few of the main pros and cons of each

- Decide which is most appropriate to C company based on information given in the pre seen and unseen

- Tailor your recommendation to the scenario – for example, explaining the exact type of cost plus approach that might work better

- I can apply risk management techniques such as sensitivity analysis and decision trees
- I can discuss risk management

Illustration – 5

Scenario/Trigger

Y company develops and manufactures a range of drugs for minor ailments. It has just launched a product which seems to cure the common cold.

Task

Evaluate the risks for Y in the context of this new venture.

Suggested Approach

- Consider the different categories of risk

- Brainstorm the most relevant for this situation using the category headings

- Try to evaluate them by looking at probability and impact

3.2 Business skills

At the management level the skills within this generic competency fall mainly within the E2 syllabus with a small amount also coming from F2 and P2. Here is a sample of the competencies which you may be expected to demonstrate:

- I can discuss developments in strategic management

- I can analyse the global business environment

- I can discuss the concepts involved in managing projects

Illustration – 6

Scenario Trigger

F company is about to embark on the implementation of a new IT system.

Task

Describe the appropriate stages in achieving a successful outcome

Suggested Approach

- Read the question carefully – this regards the implementation stage only
- Consider the main stages in implementation of new system e.g training, documentation etc
- Consider project management techniques which can be utilised
- Combine the stages, techniques and relevant points from the scenario in your answer

- I can discuss the most appropriate techniques for managing organisational relationships
- I can discuss the process of investment decision making

Illustration – 7

Scenario/Trigger

S company is considering investing in a new piece of machinery.

Task

Discuss the methods which could be used to appraise this investment.

Suggested Approach

- Consider the main techniques available – e.g. payback period and NPV

- Link the advantages and disadvantages of these techniques to information given in the scenario – e.g. if the company has liquidity problems, then this could be an argument in favour of using payback.

- I can discuss process management techniques such as TQM and JIT

e.g

Illustration – 8

Scenario/Trigger

The board of directors at A company have set a key objective to improve quality in all aspects of the organisation.

Task

Discuss suitable techniques available to achieve this objective

Suggested Approach

- List the possible quality management techniques available e.g quality circles

- Consider the advantages and disadvantages and their applicability to the information given about A company

- I can discuss the impact of the regulatory environment of an entity

3.3 People Skills

At the management level the skills within this generic competency fall mainly within the E2 syllabus with a small amount also coming from P2. Here is a sample of the competencies which you may be expected to demonstrate:

- I can discuss the concepts involved with managing people

Illustration – 9

Scenario/Trigger

Z company, a medium sized entrepreneurial organisation, has recently been taken over by a large international listed group. Concerns have been raised over how the leadership style may change as a result.

Task

Explain the leadership issues which may arise at Z company.

Suggested Approach

- Consider the leadership style before acquisition (entrepreneurial) and the attributes of such a style

- Consider the likely leadership approach taken by the group

- Discuss issues which may arise in the change from one to the other

- I can discuss the roles of communication, negotiation, influence and persuasion in the management process

- I can influence relevant stakeholders

---

e.g

Illustration – 10

Scenario/Trigger

Company G is recruiting a management accountant whose role includes giving presentations to internal customers.

Task

Explain the techniques which should be utilised to influence such stakeholders.

Suggested Approach

- List the various stakeholders who will fit under the heading 'internal customers'
- Determine their information needs and wants
- Discuss ways to influence such stakeholders and show their needs are met

---

- I can negotiate with relevant stakeholders
- I can assist in effective decision making within the organisation
- I can communicate effectively with relevant stakeholders

Illustration – 11

Scenario/Trigger

B company will shortly close operations in one European country as it is moving manufacturing to Asia.

Task

Identify the stakeholder groups which need to be informed and discuss appropriate methods of communication for each group identified

Suggested Approach

- Brainstorm stakeholder groups
- Decide which groups will have an interest in this decision
- Consider possible communication methods e.g email, letter, meeting
- Based on importance and sensitivity of stakeholder, determine most appropriate communication method for each

---

- I can collaborate with relevant stakeholders

3.4 Leadership Skills

At the management level the skills within this generic competency fall mainly within the E2 syllabus with a small amount also coming from P2. Here is a sample of the competencies which you may be expected to demonstrate:

- I can build an effective team by considering the issues associated with building, leading and managing teams

---

Illustration – 12

Scenario/Trigger

C company offers a range of financial training products across several sites in a large European city. Some members of staff are based in one location all the time and others travel to each site to deliver training and support students.

Task

Discuss the team management issues arising from this situation.

Suggested Approach

- Try to put yourself in the situation of the team members – what would your concerns be?
- Try to put yourself in the situation of the team leader – what would the difficulties be?

- I can coach and mentor staff
- I can participate in driving organisational performance
- I can motivate and inspire staff

Illustration – 13

Scenario/Trigger

X company is about to embark on a comprehensive programme of system upgrades within the finance department.

Task

Draft an email explaining these changes to the department.

Suggested Approach

- Think about how these changes will affect the department – what will their main concerns be?

- What will the benefits be to the department?

- Address the above two points in your email using a positive tone

---

- I can recommend techniques to manage resistance to change

3.5 Integration marks

There are 9 marks for integration skills at the management level. These may be incorporated into the mark allocations of any of the four categories above and can involve a mixture of the following:

- Being able to see the "bigger picture" and "wider context" relating to an issue for example, the implications on the firm as a whole

- Linking discussions to each of the three underlying papers

- Linking discussions between the current and previous tasks in the exam

4 Summary

You should now have a better understand of how the technical knowledge from previous studies may translate into what you need to be able to DO in the exam in the form of competencies. You should also now recognise if it is likely that you will have some gaps in your knowledge which you will need to revisit.

Next steps:

(1) You can begin to revisit and revise technical material from your previous studies according to the summaries given in this chapter. However we suggest you continue to do this alongside working through the rest of this book so you can also learn how you may need to apply the knowledge.

(2) Remember that you are unlikely to have to perform detailed calculations in the case study exam. However you may need to explain or interpret calculations and so an appreciation of how they are prepared is still relevant and useful.

3

Integrating skills and knowledge

Chapter learning objectives

- To understand how the learning outcomes and skills derived from the individual papers are integrated within the case study competencies and tasks.

1 Triggers and tasks – integrating the skills

In the previous chapter we considered each competency in isolation. It is important that you understand how these competencies will be linked in the examination. We can now bring together these skills into a series of integrated tasks.

Consider the following short scenario:

Scenario – Company Z

Company Z manufactures a range of kitchen gadgets using advanced production line techniques in its South East Asian factory. Much of the process of manufacture is automated although reliable supervisors are required to monitor the machinery and minimise any downtime caused by faults.

The company ships the gadgets to a range of European ports and the goods are sold in high street household goods shops and also through several large online retailers.

Profits in Z have declined significantly in the past 12 months and the Board believes this may be due to uncompetitive pricing and has asked you, as the senior management accountant, to investigate.

This is an example of what CIMA refer to in the Case study exam as a **trigger**. This information and the events occurring will give rise to one or more tasks. These tasks are likely to come from a range of different generic competency areas.

Technical skills

So the first task you may be asked to complete could demonstrate your technical skills. One of the skills here is to 'advise on different methods of analysing and managing costs'. So you may be asked to do the following:

Task 1

Prepare a briefing note for the Board explaining the issues involved with the current absorption costing system and evaluate a suitable alternative.

Given the information in the trigger (and much more detailed company and environmental information provided in the pre-seen information) you are likely to conclude that a company such as Z should be using ABC to more effectively calculate full product costs and that this could have an impact on pricing.

Business Skills

As part of the business skills competency you need to show that you can 'analyse the global business environment'. This may include recognising that other factors will affect pricing and you are given the opportunity to demonstrate this understanding in the next task:

Task 2

Evaluate the external factors that Z needs to take into account when setting suitable prices.

People Skills

Another key generic competency that you will be required to demonstrate involves people skills such as the ability to 'influence relevant stakeholders'.

It is possible that you will be tested on your understanding of relevant theory and techniques explaining how to influence. However it is also likely that you will show your ability through actually influencing relevant stakeholders through the task.

So the above task could be rewritten as:

Task 2 – Version 2

Write a report for the Board which sets out your advice on the appropriate basis for pricing at Z.

Your report should include an evaluation of the external factors which Z needs to take into account when setting suitable prices.

Leadership skills

The final generic competency is leadership.

As with people skills there is knowledge which you may have to show and apply in the case study, for example showing you can 'recommend techniques to manage resistance to change'.

So you may be required to complete the following task:

Task 3
Discuss the impact on the organisation of moving towards an ABC system and evaluate how such a change may be managed.

This tests your knowledge and application of change management techniques. Leadership also includes skills such as an ability to 'motivate and inspire staff'.

With this in mind you may also have to demonstrate leadership through completion of a task such as:

Task 4
Write a letter to the employees of Z explaining the move towards an ABC system, clearly showing the reasons for the move and the likely impact it will have on the staff and the organisation

So to summarise the progression here:

> Prepare a briefing note for the Board explaining the issues involved with the current absorption costing system and evaluate a suitable alternative.

Do accounting and finance work

↓

> Write a report for the Board which sets out your advice on the appropriate basis for pricing at Z. Your report should include an evaluation of the external factors which Z needs to take into account when setting suitable process.

In the context of the business

↓

> Discuss the impact on the organisation of moving towards an ABC system and evaluate how such a change can be managed.

To influence people

↓

> Write a letter to the employees of Z explaining the mover towards an ABC system, clearly showing the reasons for the move and the likely impact it will have on the staff and the organisation.

And lead within the organisation

2 Triggers and tasks – integrating the technical syllabi

As well as integrating the competencies it is useful to understand how the different technical papers on which the case study builds (E2, P2 and F2) are integrated in the exam.

The above series of tasks can be mapped out as follows:

	P2	E2	F2
Technical skills	(1) Explain the issues involved with the current absorption costing system and evaluate a suitable alternative. (2) Advise on the appropriate basis for pricing at Z		
Business skills		(2) Evaluate the external factors which Z needs to take into account when setting suitable prices.	
People skills		(3) Discuss the impact on the organisation of moving towards an ABC system and evaluate how such a change may be managed.	

Leadership skills		(4) Explain the move towards an ABC system to the employees, clearly showing the reasons for the move and the likely impact it will have on the staff and the organisation	

As you can see this series of tasks does not contain any skills from F2. The exam weightings for the case study are based on the competencies rather than the syllabi.

Let's look at another scenario:

Company P is a multi-channel retailer based in a large European country with stores across the continent as well as a significant online presence. As part of a planned expansion plan P has identified a potential takeover target, Company Q.

Company Q operates a series of retail outlets across the east coast of the United States selling clothes and homewares. It has previously attempted, unsuccessfully, to launch a luxury food range. Company Q is considered financially secure due to the fact that the majority of its retail premises are owned rather than leased.

A similar series of tasks to the first example, incorporating a different range of technical content, could be mapped as follows:

	P2	E2	F2
Technical skills			(4) A business valuation has been prepared using discounted cash flows. Evaluate the use of the company WACC in this situation.
Business skills	(1) Explain the relevant steps which need to be followed to ensure an appropriate long term investment decision is made		
People skills		(3) Discuss techniques which can be used in negotiating a suitable purchase price for this company with the vendor	

Leadership skills	(2)	Evaluate the extent to which this acquisition will drive performance within the organisation		

3 Summary

You should now appreciate how the different technical areas from previous studies may integrate and form more complex triggers and tasks. You should also understand how you may see progression through the four generic competency areas.

Next steps:

(1) Return to the previous chapter and consider the range of competency statements which we gave you. Can you create your own integrated tasks using skills from each of the technical syllabi?

(2) Think about your own role at work. Where do you use technical skills? What about Business skills? Do you have much opportunity to use People skills or even Leadership? Thinking about your own experiences is very useful in generating ideas in the exam.

chapter

4

Preseen information for the pilot case

Chapter learning objectives

1 Introduction

The Case Study Examinations are like no other CIMA exam; there is no new syllabus to study or formulae to learn. The best way to be successful at this level is to practise using past case study exams and mock exams based on your real live case study. By reviewing previous case studies alongside your current case you will improve your commercial thought processes and will be more aware of what the examiner expects. By sitting mock exams, under timed conditions you can hone your exam techniques and, in particular, your time management skills.

This textbook is therefore based on this principle. It presents the pilot case study and uses this to demonstrate the skills and techniques that you must master to be successful. The first pilot case, Flyjet, will be used to walkthrough the processes and approach. The remainder of this chapter contains the Flyjet pre-seen material.

We would advise that you skim read this now before moving on to Chapter 5 where you will be provided with more guidance on how to familiarise yourself with the pre-seen material.

2 Reference Material – 1

Introduction

Fly-jet is one of several low-cost airlines operating in Western and Southern Europe. It is classified as a "short-haul" carrier, operating flights to major European cities and tourist resorts. By definition, such airlines offer flights with duration of three hours or less. Typically, short-haul flights use small to medium-sized planes, with seating capacities ranging from 40 to 180 passengers.

Fly-jet's business model is based on the low-cost model first introduced by Southwest airlines in the USA. This model aims to provide customers with a basic service at the lowest possible price. Airlines such as Fly-jet are often referred to as "no-frills" because they have eliminated many of the services and facilities that their more traditional competitors offer in order to undercut their prices.

For example:

- Fly-jet often uses regional airports that are smaller and further from major cities, but which charge lower landing fees than major airports.

- Fly-jet does not provide passengers with free in-flight snacks and refreshments. Instead, it sells drinks and sandwiches during flights.

- All of Fly-jet's ticket sales are made through the company's website. That avoids paying commission to travel agents.

- Fly-jet's tickets are for designated flights and cannot be changed. If a customer wishes to travel on a different flight after making a booking then it is necessary to buy a new ticket. Traditional airlines often offer some flexibility in bookings.

- Passengers are issued with boarding cards that do not assign them to specific seats on the aircraft. That encourages passengers to board quickly, thereby reducing the costs associated with delays.

- All fares are "point-to-point". Customers cannot buy connecting flights. Customers may wish to travel from City A to City C but be unable to find a direct flight. A no-frills airline that had flights from City A to City B and City B to City C would sell the customer two separate tickets and would take no responsibility if the first flight was late and the customer missed the second flight to City C as a result. Traditional airlines generally sell connecting flights as a package and accept full responsibility for getting passengers to their final destinations.

- No-frills airlines also tend to operate a single model of aircraft. That leads to a number of efficiencies. For example, pilots are qualified to operate specific models of aircraft. Each of Fly-jet's pilots is qualified to fly all of the company's planes. Inventories of parts are streamlined by the fact that there is only one model of plane and all of Fly-jet's engineers are qualified to maintain that model.

Markets and economics

When Fly-jet was first established it tended to attract mainly private individuals who wished to travel for leisure or for personal reasons. Fly-jet and the other no-frills airlines created their own customer base of travellers who would possibly have travelled by rail or might simply not have travelled at all.

The success of the no-frills airlines has had a number of quite significant effects. One of the most notable has been the development of many of the regional airports that are served by these airlines. In particular, many now have excellent bus and rail links to nearby cities and have become far more attractive to customers, particularly business travellers. That has stimulated demand for landing slots at these airports, which has led to increased landing charges. That has reduced the cost savings associated with operating out of these airports in comparison to the airports used by the traditional full-service airlines.

These improved transport links have encouraged many business customers to travel by no-frills airlines. In some cases it is actually more convenient to travel via these regional airports because they are smaller and their owners are keen to ensure that the service that is offered exceeds that of the major hub airports. It is increasingly difficult to justify paying more for a ticket from a full-service airline when the basic service offered by the no-frills airlines is just as good.

These changes have led to prices charged by no-frills airlines increasing due to higher costs of operating from airports and also because of greater demand for seats. At the same time, many of the traditional airlines have cut their prices in order to retain customers. That has led to them copying some of the no-frills airlines' innovations, such as online ticket sales. Conversely, some of the no-frills airlines have started to offer some of the services that have traditionally been restricted to the full-service airlines. For example, some of these airlines assign seats at check-in, making it easier for customers to ensure that they can sit beside their travelling companions. Fly-jet has, to date, resisted the temptation to incur additional expense in order to enhance passenger comfort.

On a macroeconomic level the on-going recession in the Eurozone has reduced demand for travel, both by individuals and by business customers. That has forced all airlines to focus on their costs and to maintain customer loyalty.

Many airlines, including Fly-jet and other low-cost operators, have tried to gain extra revenue by offering related services. These include the offer of services such as car hire, insurance and accommodation through partner organisations. There has also been a policy of 'unbundling' services with separate charges for priority boarding, additional luggage and credit and debit card fees.

Job Description

You are the senior management accountant. Your main role in the organisation is to provide information to the Finance Director to enable the company's performance to be measured and for decision making purposes.

3 Reference Material – 2

Flyjet Costing information

In common with the remainder of the airline industry, Fly-jet benchmarks its costs on the basis of the cost per available seat kilometre (ASK). For example, if a plane with 100 seats flies over a 700 kilometre route then the cost will be divided by $100 \times 700 = 70,000$ to give a number of cents per ASK.

Fly-jet's most direct competitor is National Air, a full-service airline that is based in Fly-jet's home country. The two airlines compete directly on several key routes. Both airlines use similarly sized aircraft, although Fly-jet's planes always have more seats because Fly-jet does not have to make provision for carrying and serving in-flight meals.

Fly-jet has estimated National Air's ASK in comparison to its own as follows:

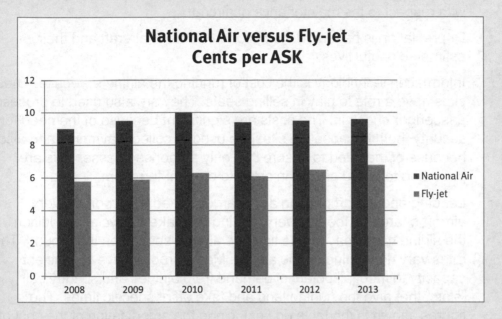

These costs have been analysed for 2013:

	National Air	Fly-jet
Fuel	1.8	1.7
Staff costs	1.7	1.2
Engineering	1.4	1.4
Depreciation	1.2	1.0
Information technology	1.0	0.9
Landing and airport parking	1.2	0.8
In-flight meals	1.3	(0.2)
	9.6	6.8

These are the direct costs associated with actually operating the flights.

- Fuel is the cost of aviation fuel used by aircraft.

- Staff costs include all costs associated with employing flight crew and also the staff employed at airports who are involved in assisting passengers and managing flight operations.

- Engineering costs include the costs of wages and parts used in maintaining and servicing aircraft and also in the inspection of aircraft before flights. Both National Air and Fly-jet have excellent reputations with respect to the maintenance of aircraft.

- Depreciation is based on the historical costs of aircraft and their estimated useful lives.

- Information technology is the cost of running the airline's website. These sites have a role to play in selling seats. They are also used to process passenger check-in. The costs are significant because of the need for security, both because the sites are used to collect payments and also because of the need to ensure that only authorised passengers are permitted to board aircraft in order to prevent terrorism.

- Landing and airport parking are charges levied by airports. Every airport charges a fee for every landing and take-off cycle. In addition, the airline has to pay for the time the aircraft spends on the ground. The rates vary depending on the airport. Many airports have insufficient capacity to meet all potential demand from airlines and so they sell "slots" that give the right to land and take off at specific times. The figures shown in the table do not include the amortisation of the cost of purchased airport slots.

- National Air provides its customers with in-flight meals as part of its service. Fly-jet's in-flight meals are sold to customers and the resulting contribution is shown here for the sake of comparability.

These costs are based on available seats per kilometre.

National Air's flights generally operate at an average utilisation rate of 75% whereas Fly-jet's operate at an average of 86%. Fly-jet's utilisation rate used to be much higher, but the airline expanded its fleet as demand grew and then faced a decline in demand, partly because of the recession and partly because the full-service airlines started to reduce their ticket prices.

The three key issues in running a no-frills airline are:

- Cost

- Utilisation

- Revenue maximisation

Fly-jet has a reputation for cutting costs to the bare minimum in every area except for safety and aircraft maintenance. The airline's management accountants conduct regular zero-based budgeting (ZBB) reviews, in consultation with other managers, in every area. That has led to some very significant changes over the years. For example, Fly-jet used to have a call centre so that customers could buy tickets over the telephone. That was closed down when it became commonplace for potential customers to have access to the internet and so Fly-jet switched to the exclusive use of its website for ticket sales.

Utilisation is important because empty seats generate no revenue. The variable cost of each additional passenger is close to zero. Fly-jet studies the occupancy rates of flights very closely. The airline aims to fill at least 90% of seats. When occupancy levels decrease it is sometimes possible to stimulate demand through marketing. For example, emails can be sent out to encourage customers to fly to that destination. Fly-jet also reduces the frequency of flights on unpopular routes. In extreme cases, the route will be abandoned altogether. The airline will only reduce ticket prices as a last resort, perhaps because a competitor is consistently charging less. Lower prices can stimulate demand, but is potentially harmful with respect to revenue generation.

Fly-jet maximises its revenues by varying ticket prices in accordance with a complicated statistical analysis of demand. For example, flights in the early morning and late evening are frequently more expensive than those during the day because business travellers are more likely to travel at those times and are less concerned about price. The timing of a ticket purchase can also be significant. Customers who book early tend to pay less than those who wait until just before the departure date because those who book close to departure will generally have less choice about when they fly and so Fly-jet can charge them more. Fly-jet also studies competing airlines' ticket prices constantly by logging on to their websites.

4 Reference Material – 3

Fly-jet fleet

Fly-jet operates a fleet of 74 of one model of aircraft. That model of aircraft is used by many airlines, both no-frills and full-service.

The manufacturer builds the aircraft to order. The basic airframe, engines and cockpit are identical in every case, although customers can specify the layout of the interior, subject to meeting all relevant health and safety requirements.

Fly-jet specifies a very functional interior. Its aircraft do not have galleys for the preparation of in-flight meals because snacks and drinks are sold from trolleys that are stocked and loaded on to the aircraft at the airport. Other airlines usually have three toilets on each plane, but Fly-jet only has two. These changes give space for more seats than the full-service operators.

Fly-jet's aircraft do not have window blinds in order to reduce the cost of maintenance and cleaning. They also have non-reclining seats, again to reduce maintenance and to make it possible to squeeze in an additional row of seats.

Fly-jet has been approached by their aircraft manufacturer's largest competitor. The competitor has offered to replace Fly-jet's fleet with a new aircraft that it is presently designing. Fly-jet has been provided with the following estimated costing:

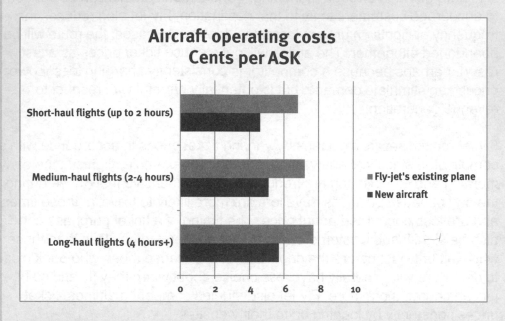

5 Reference Material – 4

Stock market information

Fly-jet's share price has stagnated in recent years. The airline has struggled to maintain growth in the face of stiff competition and a declining demand.

6 Reference Material – 5

Flyjet Board of Directors

Executive Directors

Aileen Adams, Chief Executive Officer (aged 62)

Aileen Adams has spent her entire working life in the aviation industry. She has held senior management roles with two other airlines, generally in the areas of planning and marketing.

Aileen joined Fly-jet in 1997, becoming Marketing Director in 2001. She was subsequently promoted to CEO in 2007

Charles Brown, Marketing Director (aged 57)

Charles Brown joined Fly-jet in 1996. Previously, he worked in a major retail organisation.

Charles joined the board in 2002. Since then he has been instrumental in designing the company's marketing strategy, with particular emphasis on the promotion of 'no-frills' as an alternative to traditional airlines.

Simone Connelly, Finance Director, (aged 54)

Simone Connelly is a qualified accountant. She has worked in a wide variety of organisations, including a period in the public sector.

At Fly-jet, Simone has been involved in the development of the information systems that are now the basis of the company's online sales and management control.

Patrick Dunlop, Human Resources Director (aged 61)

Patrick Dunlop was a senior personnel manager in a variety of organisations before joining Fly-jet in 2000. He was initially responsible for the recruitment and training of cabin crew.

He was promoted to Deputy Director of Human Resources in 2006 and became Human Resources Director in 2011.

Independent Non-Executive Directors

Executive Directors

Marie Elder, Chairman and Senior Independent Non-Executive Director (aged 63)

Marie Elder was formerly chairman of Harrison Boyle, a major quoted retailer. She has been chairman and senior independent director of Fly-jet since 2012.

Marie chairs Fly-jet's Nomination and Remuneration Committees. She is a qualified accountant and also serves as a trustee of a major charity.

Gary Foster, Independent Non-Executive Director (aged 65)

Gary Foster has enjoyed a distinguished career in the retail industry, having held directorships at a succession of three large corporations, latterly as chief executive of Squire. Gary is a member of the Audit and Remuneration Committees.

Lydia Galbraith, Independent Non-Executive Director (aged 60)

Lydia Galbraith is currently Pro-Chancellor and Chairman of the Board of Governors of Capital University. She is Chairman of Milo, a quoted publishing company. She sits on the Nomination and Audit Committees.

Peter Harvey, Independent Non-Executive Director (aged 64)

Peter Harvey was previously Chief Executive of Central Airport Group, a quoted company that owns and operates several major airports. Peter is a member of both the Remuneration and Audit Committees.

7 Reference Material – 6

Risks

Description of risk	Potential impact	Changes since last year	Mitigation
Safety and security			
An aircraft could crash because of a malfunction.	Significant damage to Fly-jet's reputation and exposure to potential claims for compensation.	unchanged	Aircraft are maintained to the highest standard, in accordance with manufacturer's recommendations.
Terrorist activity could lead to the death or injury of passengers and loss of aircraft.	Reputational damage and potential criminal sanctions and/or civil penalties.	unchanged	Fly-jet works closely with all relevant agencies and the security departments at all airports.
Economic environment			
Economic conditions may discourage expenditure on business and leisure travel.	Revenues may decline and utilisation rates may become uneconomic	unchanged	Fly-jet monitors all relevant economic variables.
Competition			
Fly-jet operates in highly competitive markets.	Market share could decline in the face of competition.	unchanged	Fly-jet has a strong market presence and has a loyal customer base of frequent travellers.
Environment			
Environmental legislation may be tightened in the face of concerns about emissions and consumption of fossil fuels.	Revenues may decline.	unchanged	Fly-jet operates a modern and efficient fleet of aircraft that comply with all current and foreseeable emissions requirements.

IT systems			
Fly-jet relies totally on its IT systems for the operation of its business.	Any failure could disrupt operations and cost revenues.	unchanged	A full suite of security and backup systems is in place to prevent the loss of systems or data.
People			
Fly-jet requires a full complement of highly trained and qualified staff.	Operations would be disrupted by a shortage of pilots, cabin crew or engineering staff	unchanged	Fly-jet offers a competitive reward package and maintains a close relationship with employee representatives.

8 Reference Material – 7

Corporate Social Responsibility

Safety

Fly-jet regards passenger safety as absolutely paramount. The airline is totally committed to providing a safe and secure service that protects customers, staff, aircraft and the company's reputation.

Fly-jet has systems in place to monitor and promote safety. These ensure that:

- staff at all levels are aware of their responsibilities with respect to safety

- the company's culture stresses the need for safety at all times

- staff are provided with the training and equipment that they require

- risks are identified and managed

- contingency plans are in place to deal with the effects of accidents

Fly-jet has a Safety Committee that is chaired by a member of the board. That committee meets regularly in order to review the operations of all processes and procedures that relate to safety.

There is a Safety Department that monitors and coordinates all safety activity across the company. Every member of staff is encouraged to contact the Safety Department to report any matters that arise. The Safety Department has an operations centre that is staffed 24 hours a day. The Safety Department is authorised to take any action that is necessary to address any safety-related matter.

Fly-jet is subjects to stringent safety requirements imposed by national and international regulators.

Environment

Fly-jet accepts that human activity, including air travel, contributes to the consumption of scarce natural resources and the emission of CO_2 and other pollutants. As a major airline we are willing to accept that we have a direct responsibility to minimise our impact on the environment. We take that responsibility seriously.

Fly-jet has invested heavily in a modern fleet of aircraft that are designed to be fuel-efficient and to minimise pollution. These aircraft are also designed to be as quiet as possible in order to minimise the disruption to residents who live close to the airports from which we

People

The airline industry is essentially a service industry. Customers will only feel valued and comfortable if the company's staff are committed to providing them with excellent service.

Fly-jet's places considerable emphasis on recruitment and training. The company has a training facility for cabin staff and our training programme is recognised as one of the best in the industry.

We offer a competitive rewards package and we monitor staff morale closely. We are careful to retain staff and conduct detailed exit interviews with those who resign. We act quickly to deal with threats such as improved conditions offered by our competition.

Fly-jet works closely with unions and other employee representatives to ensure that any concerns are explored and addressed as quickly and effectively as possible.

Fly-jet has come through a difficult period, during which it was necessary to make cuts in staffing levels. We did our utmost to minimise compulsory redundancies. That process of rightsizing has now concluded and we hope that there will be a period of stability, followed by an increase in staffing levels in line with the anticipated economic recovery.

9 Reference Material – 8

Flyjet

Extracts from Financial Statements

Fly-jet

Consolidated income statement for the year ended 31 March 2015

	Notes	2015	2014
		$m	$m
Revenue		1,858	1,672
Staff costs		(268)	(228)
Fuel		(276)	(215)
Airport charges		(248)	(179)
Ground operations		(172)	(165)
Maintenance		(76)	(74)
Depreciation and amortisation		(726)	(698)
Marketing		(52)	(48)
Restructing costs	**(1)**	(36)	–
Other operating expenses	**(2)**	(64)	(48)
Operating (loss)/profit		(60)	17
Finance costs		(4)	(5)
Profit/(Loss) before tax		(64)	12
Tax expense		(2)	(10)
Loss of year		(66)	2

Fly-jet

Consolidated statement of changes in equity for the year ended 31 March 2015

	Share capital	Share premium	Retained earnings	Total equity
	$m	$m	$m	
Balance as at 31 March 2014	700	400	141	1,241
Loss for the year	–	–	(66)	(66)
Balance as at 31 March 2015	700	400	75	1,175

Fly-jet

Consolidated statement of financial position for the year ended 31 March 2015

	Notes	2015	2014
		$m	$m
Non-current assets			
Intangible assets	(4)	114	113
Property, plant and equipment	(5)	1,443	2,194
Current assets			
Inventory		8	7
Trade receivables		91	98
Cash		11	16
		110	121
		1,667	2,428

Equity

Share capital	700	700
Share premium	400	400
Retained earnings	75	141
	1,175	1,241

Non-current liabilities

Borrowings	395	1,000
Deferred tax	3	6
	398	1,006

Current liabilities

Trade payables	94	81
	1,667	2,328

Fly-jet

Consolidated Statement of Cash flows for the year ended 31 March 2015

	2015	2014
	$m	$m
Cash flows from operating activities		
Cash receipts from customers	1,851	1,947
Cash paid to suppliers and employees	(1113)	(1,072)
Cash generated from operations	738	875
Income taxes paid	(6)	(13)
Net cash from operating activities	732	862

Cash flows investing activities

Purchase of property, plant and equipment	(64)	(875)
Purchase of non-current intangibles	(6)	
Proceeds from disposal of property, plant and equipment	41	2
Proceeds from disposal of non-current intangibles	1	
Net cash used in investing activities	(28)	(873)

Cash flows from financing activities

Interest paid	(4)	(5)
Loan repayment	(705)	
Dividend paid		(5)
Net cash used in financing activities	(709)	(10)
Net increase/(decrease) in cash and cash equivalents	(5)	(21)
Cash and cash equivalents at beginning of period	16	37
Cash and cash equivalents at end of period	11	16

Notes

(1) Restructuring costs

  During the year Fly-jet ceased all operations from West Airport.

  This necessitated the payment of $24m in compensation to various counterparties for the cancellation of various contractual commitments associated with Fly-jet's operations. Fly-jet also had to make 200 staff redundant at a cost of $12m.

(2) Operating expenses

Other operating expenses include:

	2015	2014
	$m	$m
Losses on disposal of intangible assets	2	–
Losses on disposal of property, plant and equipment	48	37
Operating lease charges on aircraft	10	1

(3) Tax expense

	2015	2014
	$m	$m
Current tax	5	11
Reversal on deferred tax	(3)	(1)
Tax expense	2	10

(4) Intangible assets

	Goodwill	Landing slots	Total
	$m	$m	$m
Cost at April 2014	100	20	120
Additions	–	6	6
Disposals		(4)	(4)
Cost at 31 March 2015	100	12	122
Accumulated amortisation at 1 April 2014	–	7	7
Charge for year	–	2	2
Disposals	–	(1)	(1)
Accumulated amortisation at 31 March 2015	–	8	8
Net book value at 31 March 2015	100	4	114
Net book value at 1 April 2014	100	3	113

(5) Property, plant and equipment

	Property	Plant and equipment	Total
	$m	$m	$m
Cost at April 2014	46	4,440	4,486
Additions	–	64	64
Disposals		(187)	(187)
Cost at 31 March 2015	46	4,317	4,363
Accumulated amortisation at 1 April 2014	14	2,278	2,292
Charge for year	2	724	726
Disposals	–	(98)	(98)
Accumulated amortisation at 31 March 2015	16	2,904	2,920
Net book value at 31 March 2015	30	1,413	1,443
Net book value at 1 April 2014	32	2,162	2,194

10 Reference Material – 9

National Air

Extracts from Financial Statements

National Air

Consolidated income statement for the year ended 31 March 2015

	Notes	2015 $m	2014 $m
Revenue		12,018	10,450
Staff costs		(2,587)	(2,192)
Fuel		(2,167)	(1,935)
Airport changes		(3,185)	(2,722)
Ground operations		(1,324)	(1,204)
Maintenance		(544)	(499)
Depreciation and amortisation		0	
Marketing		(982)	(808)
Other operating expenses		(84)	(87)
Operating profit		1,145	1,003
Finance costs		(10)	(10)
Loss before tax		1,135	993
Tax expenses		(254)	(230)
Profit for year		881	763

National Air

Consolidated statement of financial position as at 31 March 2015

	2015 $m	2014 $m
Non-current assets		
Intangible assets	2,000	1,800
Property, plant and equipment	4,270	3,950
	6,270	5,750
Current assets		
Inventory	24	21
Trade receivables	197	186
Cash	28	23
	249	230
	6,519	5,980
Equity		
Share premium	300	300
Retained earnings	425	367
	1,925	1,867
Non-current liabilities		
Borrowings	4,389	3,923
Deferred tax	18	12
	4,407	3,935
Current liabilities		
Trade payables	187	178
	6,519	5,980

11 Summary

We are now working through the Pilot exam from beginning to end so you can see all of the skills and techniques which may be required in this exam. This chapter simply reproduces the pre-seen information for the Pilot exam and we will work through this in more detail in the next two chapters.

Next steps:

(1) Make sure you have at least skim read the pre-seen before moving on to Chapter Five where we will consider how to do further analysis.

(2) It might be useful to make a list at this point of what you think some of the relevant technical areas might be – are you comfortable with these areas?

Analysing the pre-seen

Chapter learning objectives

- to understand various techniques and models that can help familiarisation with the pre-seen.

1 The importance of familiarisation

The pre-seen material is released approximately seven weeks before you sit the exam and one of your first tasks will be to analyse the context within which the case is set. Although your responses in the exam will be driven by the unseen material, you will only be able to fully assess the impact of each event on the organisation if you have a sufficient depth of knowledge and awareness of both the organisation and the industry in which it operates.

The purpose of the pre-seen material is to allow you to gain that knowledge and awareness. Remember, you will be acting in the position of a management accountant who works for the organisation in a manager role. It will therefore be expected that you will have the same level of familiarisation as someone fulfilling that role.

It is extremely important that you study the pre-seen material thoroughly before you go into the examination. There are two main reasons for this:

- It will save time in the examination itself if you are already familiar with the pre-seen material.

- It enables you to develop a view of the situation facing the organisation in the case study.

You will not be able to respond to the examination tasks from the pre-seen material alone; the unseen material given to you in the examination will present significant new information that may alter the situation substantially. Even so, a major step towards success in the examination is a careful study, exploration and understanding of the pre-seen material.

Each set of pre-seen material is different but as a general rule, you can expect the following:

- Industry background

- History of the business

- Key personnel

- Current business/industry issues

- Financial Statements

Each of these areas will need reviewing in detail.

You should question what each piece of information tells you, and why the examiner may have given it to you.

2 Exhibit by exhibit analysis

The purpose of this initial stage is to lay a foundation for further analysis. It's more about asking questions than finding solutions. Before you do anything else, you should read the pre-seen material from beginning to end without making any notes, simply to familiarise yourself with the scenario.

Read the material again, as many times as you think necessary, without making notes. You can do this over a period of several days, if you wish.

When you think you are reasonably familiar with the situation described by the material, you should start to make notes. By making notes, you will become more familiar with the detail of the scenario.

- Try to make notes on each paragraph (or each group of short paragraphs) in the pre-seen material.

- Think about what the paragraph is telling you, and consider why this information might be of interest or relevance.

- Ask yourself "why might the examiner have told me this?".

- Try to make your questions as broad as possible; consider as many different stakeholders as possible and try to put yourself in different positions (say the CEO, a key customer, a franchise operator etc) to consider the information from different perspectives.

e.g Illustration 1 – Flyjet: Introductory overview

Given below is an example of some questions you could ask yourself relating to the first exhibit of the Management case Study pilot exam pre-seen information.

Question	Potential Response
What is the significance of being told Flyjet is a 'no-frills' airline?	• A no-frills airline will compete primarily on price, targeting customers who are looking for the cheapest flight options. • As the prices are kept as low as possible, it is important that costs are minimised – hence the lack of services such as on-board catering, free luggage allowance and larger, comfortable seats. • If costs are not kept down, then the company risks being 'stuck in the middle' and not generating sufficient profits.

How has the economic environment affected the demand for flights?	• Recession in many countries across the world has changed the habits of many business users and reduced the demand for air travel as more businesses cut back on face to face meetings. However for essential short haul business travel there is likely to be a move from full service airlines towards the no frills option.
	• The demand for leisure travel has also fallen with many consumers now opting for a 'staycation' as the levels of disposable income fall. It is also the case that some travellers who would previously have opted for long haul destinations have shifted to shorter haul holidays to keep the costs down.
List the factors which customers will consider when choosing a no-frills airline.	• PRICE
	• PRICE
	• PRICE!!!
	• And price includes administrative fees, baggage fees and credit card fees as well as the flight cost
	• Also choice of routes as some of the lower cost airlines fly to less central locations and so transfers can add to the overall cost
	• Some level of service is becoming increasingly important for no frills airline users – e.g. choice of seats

3 Note Taking

When you're making notes, try to be as creative as possible. Psychologists tell us that using conventional linear notes on their own use only a small part of our mental capacity. They are hard to remember and prevent us from drawing connections between topics. This is because they seek to classify things under hierarchical headings.

Here are some techniques that candidates find useful. See which ones work for you as you practise on the pilot case in this text.

Spider diagrams

Spider diagrams (or clustering diagrams) are a quick graphic way of summarising connections between subjects.

You cannot put much detail into a spider diagram, just a few key words. However, it does help you to 'visualise' the information in the case material.

You must expect to update your spider diagram as you go along and to redraft it when it starts to get too messy. It is all part of the learning process.

Timelines

Timelines are valuable to make sense of the sequence of events in the pre-seen and to understand where the company in the case study presently stands. The case study exam takes place in real time, so you need to be clear how long is likely to elapse between the data in the pre-seen and the actual exam. This is the time period during which the issues facing the company can be incorporated into the unseen material.

The case writer is not trying to trick you or spring something entirely unexpected on you, but you need to be aware of the timeframe and the changes that have already occurred in the company's history, so that you can offer realistic advice for the company's future.

Organisation charts

Preparing an organisation chart will familiarise you with the roles and the overlaps, and also help you to identify gaps or ambiguities in roles, as well as helping you to remember the names and roles of the key people in the case. In some cases this will be provided for you; where it isn't, you may want to draw one out.

Post-it-notes

Post-it-notes can be used to stick onto each page of the printed pre-seen material and to jot key points on. Additionally, you may want to keep a post it note for each person, and as you work through the pre-seen material. You could even stick the notes on your desk, a notice board or wall so that you can keep glancing at them to remember who's who in the case and what issues and problems have been identified. You could also jot down your ideas for alternative directions that the company could take, to prepare you for exam day.

Colours

Colours help you remember things you may want to draw upon in the exam room. You could write down all your financial calculations and observations in green whilst having red for organisational and blue for strategic. Some candidates use different colour highlighter pens to emphasise different aspects of the pre-seen material perhaps using the same colour coding suggestion.

Additionally, sometimes making notes in different colours helps you to remember key facts and some of the preparation that you have done using the pre-seen material.

Use whatever colours work for you – but it does help to make notes on both the pre-seen material and the research you do. DO NOT just read the material – you must take notes (in whatever format) and if colours help you to understand and link your research together then use colours.

4 Technical Analysis

Now you're reasonably familiar with the material it's time to carry out some technical analysis to help you identify and understand the issues facing the company.

A good starting point is to revise any 'technical' topics that might be relevant. The pre-seen material might make a reference to a particular 'technical' issue, such as the balanced scorecard approach, corporate governance requirements, internal controls, the use of derivative instruments, company valuations, and so on.

If you have forgotten about any topic that might be relevant, go back to your previous study materials and revise it.

5 Financial Analysis

You will almost certainly be given some figures in the pre-seen material. These might relate to the company's profits or losses, or product profitability. There might be statements of profit and loss and statements of financial position for previous years, future business plans, cash flow statements, capital expenditure plans, EPS and share price information and so on.

A key part of your initial analysis will be to perform some simple financial analysis, such as financial ratio calculations or a cash flow analysis. These might give you a picture of changes in profitability, liquidity, working capital management, return on capital, financial structure or cash flows over time, and will help ensure you have a rounded picture of the organisation's current position.

If a cash flow statement is not provided, it may be worth preparing a summary of cash flows. You may have to make some assumptions if the detailed information isn't provided but even with these, there is great value in appreciating where the money has come from, and where it is being spent.

Profitability ratios

You might find useful information from an analysis of profit/sales ratios, for:

- the company as a whole
- each division, or
- each product or service.

Profit margins can be measured as a net profit percentage and as a gross profit percentage. You can then look at trends in the ratios over time, or consider whether the margins are good or disappointing.

Analysing the ratio of certain expenses to sales might also be useful, such as the ratio of administration costs to sales, sales and marketing costs to sales or R&D costs to sales. Have there been any noticeable changes in these ratios over time and, if so, is it clear why the changes have happened?

Liquidity ratios

The two main measures of liquidity are:

- the current ratio (= ratio of current assets: current liabilities)
- the quick ratio or acid test ratio (= ratio of current assets excluding inventory: current liabilities).

The purpose of a liquidity ratio is to assess whether the organisation is likely to be able to pay its liabilities, when they fall due for payment, out of its operational cash flows. The current ratio is probably more useful when inventory is fairly liquid and inventory turnover is fast. The quick ratio or acid test ratio is a better measure of liquidity when inventory turnover is slow.

Check these ratios for any significant change over time, or for the possibility of poor liquidity. As a very rough guide, a current ratio below 2:1 and a quick ratio below 1:1 might be low. However, the liquidity ratios are only likely to be of significance for the case study when the ratios get very low, or the deterioration in the ratios is very large. For example, if a company has current liabilities in excess of its current assets, a liquidity problem would seem likely.

Working capital ratios

Working capital ratios can be calculated to assess the efficiency of working capital management (= management of inventory, trade receivables and trade payables). They can also be useful for assessing liquidity, because excessive investment in working capital ties up cash and slows the receipt of cash.

The main working capital ratios are:

- 'inventory days' or the average turnover period for inventory: a long period might indicate poor inventory management

- 'receivables days' or the average time that customers take to pay: a long period could indicate issues with the collection of cash, although would need to consider this in light of the entity's credit terms and industry averages.

- 'payables days' or the average time to pay suppliers: a long period could indicate cash flow difficulties for the entity, although would need to consider in light of credit terms.

You should be familiar with these ratios and how to calculate the length of the cash cycle or operating cycle.

Financial structure ratios

You might be required to consider methods of funding in your case study examination. If a company plans to expand in the future, where will the funds come from?

- Additional debt finance might only be possible if the current debt levels are not high, and financial gearing is fairly low. (The interest cover ratio is also a useful measure of debt capacity. It is the ratio of profit before interest and tax to interest costs. When the ratio is low, possibly less than 3, this could indicate that the company already has as much debt capital as it can safely afford.)

- If a company will need additional equity finding, will internally generated profits be a sufficient source of funds or will a new share issue be necessary?

You should be able to accurately prepare gearing ratios, which is debt: debt + equity.

Cash flow analysis or funding analysis

If the main objective of a company is to maximise the wealth of its shareholders, the most important financial issues will be profitability and returns to shareholders. However, other significant issues in financial strategy are often:

- cash flows and liquidity, and
- funding

A possible cash flow problem occurs whenever the cash flows from operations do not appear to be sufficient to cover all the non-operational cash payments that the company has to make, such as spending on capital expenditure items.

An analysis of future funding can be carried out by looking at the history of changes in the statement of financial position. It is a relatively simple task to look at the growth in the company's assets over time, and at how the asset growth has been funded – by equity, long-term debt or shorter-term liabilities. If equity has funded much of the growth in assets, it might be possible to see how much of the new equity has been provided by retained profits, and how much has come from new issues of shares (indicated by an increase in the allotted share capital and share premium reserve).

It is crucial that you are able to accurately calculate and interpret the key ratios such as margins, ROCE, P/E ratios and gearing.

6 Recap of key ratio calculations

Key ratios:

Ratio	Formula
Gross profit margin (GPM)	(Gross profit/Revenue) × 100%
Net profit margin (NPM)	(Net profit/Revenue) × 100%
Operating profit margin	(Operating profit/Revenue) × 100%
Profit before tax margin	(Profit before tax/Revenue) × 100%
Return on Capital Employed (ROCE)	(Operating profit/Capital Employed) × 100%
Asset turnover	Revenue/Capital Employed
Current ratio	Current assets/Current liabilities
Quick ratio	(Current assets – Inventory)/Current liabilities
Receivables days	(Trade Receivables/Credit Sales) × 365 days
Inventory days	(Inventory/Cost of Sales) × 365 days
Payables days	(Trade Payables/Cost of Sales) × 365 days
Gearing (variant 1)	Debt/Equity
Gearing (variant 2)	Debt/(Debt + Equity)
Interest cover	Operating Profit/Finance Cost

Exercise 1 – Basic Financial Analysis

Complete the following table using the information in Chapter four. Commentary on the results can be found in Chapter six.

Ratio	2015	*Working*	2014	*Working*
Revenue growth				
Operating profit margin				
Return on Capital Employed (ROCE)				
Current ratio				
Receivables days				
Inventory days				
Payables days				
Gearing				

7 Industry analysis and research

Why is industry research important?

Remember, part of your preparatory work is to analyse the context within which the case is set. A full analysis is not possible without an understanding of the industry and research may support the information provided in the pre-seen. From this analysis, you may be better able to understand the key issues and address the requirements.

The pre-seen material usually contains a good summary of relevant information about the industry. This can be relied on as accurate at the time it is published.

You could further research the industry setting for the case you are working on so that you can develop a better understanding of the problems (and opportunities) facing companies in this industry. Hopefully, it will also stop you from making unrealistic comments in your answer on the day of the exam. Finally, there will be a strong linkage between your research of the industry and the technical analysis you will be carrying out. Industry research will allow you to add further comments in terms of:

- identifying industry lifecycle stage and the factors driving it

- identifying whether any of the five forces are strong or strengthening and the factors causing this

- considering the competitive strategies being followed by companies operating in the real world and how they are achieved (e.g. special technologies, use of brands) and whether they could be adopted by the company in the pre-seen

- identifying real world issues against the PEST framework (this may involve some basic research into the laws and technologies of the industry)

- considering the impact of globalisation on the future of the industry and on the firm in the pre-seen.

Don't think that your preparation should be limited to just looking at the industry. A wider understanding of the way business is conducted and the influence of the economic and political environments on business could be just as useful. For example, an additional factor to consider is the state of the investment markets, which will affect costs of capital and share prices.

One of the best ways to achieve this wider appreciation is to regularly read the business pages of a good national newspaper.

How to conduct industry research

One of the big problems with conducting industry research is knowing where to stop. In today's technology driven society, a wealth of information is available at your fingertips so perhaps the most important aspect when performing research is to focus on reliable sources. In order to help direct your research, think about the following sources of information:

Personal networks

Some candidates have been lucky enough to find themselves facing a set of pre seen material describing the industry they work in. In this situation, they have plenty of colleagues they can talk to about the case.

Alternatively, and depending on the industry in the Case Study, it is possible that you know someone in the business from whom you can get information. Likely contacts include:

- people who work in the industry or who have worked in it

- family members or their friends

- contacts at work who have dealings with the industry in the case

- other people sitting the case study exam, either via your tuition provider or using online forums, such as CIMAsphere.

Discussing the case and your analysis of the situation of the business with an expert will help you to test out your understanding of what is important.

Trade media and news media

A journalist is a paid professional who searches out and presents information about an industry. If you can find a trade journal for the industry in the case, it will save you a lot of searching for yourself..

Trade journals can be located in three ways:

- Visit a good newsagent. The difficulty here is that only very large industries such as accounting, financial advising, computing, music and construction provide enough customers for a newsagent to consider stocking the magazine.

- Ask someone who works in the industry for the name of the journals for the industry.

- Use the Internet. Many trade journals now have websites and, in many cases, the journals can be downloaded as PDFs. Naturally there will be restrictions on logging in if you have not paid a fee, but there is a surprising amount of free media available. The best approach is to go to a search engine and type in a search inquiry such as: 'trade magazine for [name of industry] industry' or 'articles on [name of industry or real world firm]'.

News media is more general although some quality business newspapers may carry special supplements on particular industries from time to time.

It is also very important to spend time reading the financial pages of any good newspaper, not necessarily the Financial Times. It is relevant to understand what is happening in the real world with acquisitions, mergers, down-sizing, boardroom conflicts, etc. The more widely that you read the financial press, the more it will help you to understand and fully appreciate all of the many complex factors that affect companies and the selection and implementation of their strategies.

It is also recommended that you should keep yourself updated with latest information on exchange rates, interest rates, government policies, the state of the economy, and particularly what is happening in the business sectors concerning mergers and acquisitions. The acquisition of a competitor, or a hostile takeover bid is a very important strategic move. Acquisitions happen everyday in the real world and you can familiarise yourself with how these work by reading the business press.

Obviously, news media is available in hard copy from shops but also most good newspapers have websites that give you the day's stories and also have searchable archives on past stories about the industry or specific firms within it.

Using the Internet

This is the most convenient and commonly used method of researching the industry, but as noted above, try to target the information you're looking for in order to avoid wasting time. Generally, you will be looking for the following sorts of information:

- Websites of firms similar to the one(s) in the pre-seen material. This can help you learn about the sorts of products and competitive strategies they follow and may also yield financial information that can be compared with the data in the pre-seen material.

- Trade journals of the industry in the pre-seen. This will provide information on real world environmental issues facing the business.

- Articles on the industry in journals and newspapers. These will keep you up to date on developments.

- Stock market information on the real firms.

- Financial statements of real firms (often these can be downloaded from companies' websites free of charge).

- Industry reports produced by organisations such as the DTI and the large accountancy firms, which are surprisingly common, and often available for free on the Internet, if you search well.

You could review the accounts and establish:

- typical industry working capital ratios

- typical ratios of non-current

- assets to sales

- margins

- growth rates

You could then compare the accounts with the current share price and compare the market capitalisation with the asset value, and review all the normal investment ratios. You may provide yourself with some 'normal' industry figures as a basis for any comparisons you may wish to make of the unseen material in due course. You should also review all the non-financial information provided, looking in particular for:

- new technological developments, new products

- the competitive situation

If companies can be identified that are in the same or similar industries to the industry in the case, then it is possible to gain much information from these websites.

It is not helpful, as some candidates and tutors have done, to concentrate on any one single company, however similar you believe that is to the case. The examination team have made it clear that cases are not likely to be based exclusively on just one real world company and hence data will differ from any sets of accounts that you may consider the case is based on.

Company websites of public companies in similar industries can provide the annual report and accounts, any press releases, publicity material and product descriptions, and detailed documentation on such matters as rights issues and share option schemes. Often they contain specially commissioned pieces of market research that you can download. However, it's worth remembering that this research is there to encourage investors to anticipate higher returns in the future and will tend to put an optimistic gloss on events. One very efficient way to use the internet for research is to set up Google alerts for the topics you're interested in. This will provide you with daily emails containing links to new information on your specified areas.

8 Risk Analysis

It can be a good idea to prepare a risk analysis to aid your understanding of the pre-seen. When carrying out risk analysis it is good to consider the risk, the potential impact and any possible mitigation. A good example of a risk analysis can be seen in Exhibit 6 of the Flyjet pre-seen. This type of document won't always be provided and you may need to prepare it yourself.

9 Position Audit

Once you've analysed all of the above you're ready to carry out a position audit.

CIMA defines a position audit as:

Part of the planning process which examines the current state of the entity in respect of:

- resources of tangible and intangible assets and finance

- products brands and markets

- operating systems such as production and distribution

- internal organisation

- current results

- returns to stockholders.

What you should be attempting to do is stand back so you can appreciate the bigger picture of the organisation. Within your SWOT analysis you should look for:

- Threat homing in upon weakness – the potential extinction event.

- Threat on a strength – should be able to defend against it but remember competencies slip.

- Opportunity on a strength – areas they should be able to exploit.

- Opportunity on a weakness – areas where they could exploit in the future if they can change.

In addition to preparing a SWOT analysis, it is useful to prepare a two-three page summary of your analysis. Try not to simply repeat information from the pre-seen but add value by including your thoughts on the analysis you've performed.

10 Main issues and précis

Once you've prepared your summary you are finally able to consider the key issues facing the organisation. Your conclusion on the main issues arising from the pre-seen will direct your focus and aid your understanding of issues in the exam.

Once you've got a list of the main issues, give yourself more time to think. Spend some time thinking about the case study, as much as you can. You don't have to be sitting at a desk or table to do this. You can think about the case study when you travel to work or in any spare time that you have for thinking.

- When new ideas come to you, jot them down.
- If you think of a new approach to financial analysis, carry out any calculations you think might be useful.

Remember, all of the above preparatory work enables you to feel as if you really are a management accountant working for this organisation. Without the prep, you're unlikely to be convincing in this role.

11 Summary

You should now understand what you need to do in order to familiarise yourself with the pre-seen sufficiently. Working through this chapter will produce quite detailed analysis. Chapter Six will attempt to summarise this into key conclusions.

Next steps:

(1) Ensure you have applied each stage of analysis to the Flyjet pre-seen

(2) Produce a brief summary of the key issues facing Flyjet. We will give you our opinion in the following chapter but you should write your own notes on this first.

Test your understanding answers

Exercise 1 – Basic Financial Analysis

Ratio	2015	Working	2014	Working
Revenue growth	11%	(1,858 – 1,672)/1,672	–	n/a
Operating profit margin	(3%)	(60)/1,858	1%	17/1,672
Return on Capital Employed (ROCE)	(3.8%)	(60)/(1,175 + 395)	0.8%	17/(1,241 + 1,006)
Current ratio	1.17:1	110/94	1.49:1	121/81
Receivables days	18 days	(91/1,858) × 365	21 days	(98/1,672) × 365
Inventory days	4 days	(8/772) × 365	4 days	(7/633) × 365
Payables days	44 days	(94/772) × 365	47 days	(81/633) × 365
Gearing – using Debt/(Debt + Equity)	25%	395/(395 + 1,175)	44%	1,000/(1,000 + 1,241)

Summary of the pre-seen

Chapter learning objectives

- To apply the techniques covered in the previous chapter to the pilot pre-seen

1 Introduction

In the previous chapter we showed you some techniques to help you in your analysis of the pre-seen.

Once you have completed your analysis of the pre-seen for the pilot paper you can review this chapter to ensure you have identified the key points. We will take you through each exhibit highlighting the key conclusions before bringing this together into a summary using the SWOT framework.

2 Exhibit by exhibit analysis

The key issues and conclusions that could have been brought out of the pre-seen exhibits are as follows:

Reference material 1 – An introduction to the company, market and economics of the industry

- Flyjet is a low cost short haul airline operating in Europe.

- As a low cost airline prices must be kept low and therefore cost control is crucial to maintain competitive advantage.

- Flyjet has highly streamlined operations aiming to cut all but essential costs.

- Due to recession and improvements to local transport infrastructures surrounding the smaller airports there is increased demand for low cost flights by business users.

- The gap between no frills and full service airlines is reducing in terms of service provided – leading to increasing levels of competition.

Reference material 2 – Costing information

- Costs are measured per available seat kilometre which means that not only does the total cost of the flight need to be carefully managed but also the utilisation of the available seats is measured.

- Flyjet have a greater number of available seats over which to spread the costs compared to a full service airline.

- Flyjet are therefore operating with a much lower cost per available seat kilometre than National Air – their closest competitor. This should allow them to be highly price competitive.

Cost proportions can be analysed as follows:

Cost – as % of total	National Air	Flyjet
Fuel	18.75	25.00
Staff	17.71	17.65
Engineering	14.58	20.59
Depreciation	12.50	14.70
Information Technology	10.42	13.20
Landing and airport parking	12.50	11.76
Inflight meals	13.54	12.90

Commentary:

- Flyjet obviously saves costs through not providing inflight meals but also seem to have efficiencies in staff costs and landing and airport parking. As a no frills airline with minimum turnaround times for flights they are likely to have reduced numbers of ground staff. They may also use smaller, more remote airports which will reduce the landing and airport parking costs.

- If Flyjet wish to reduce costs this may be possible with fuel. Maintaining the level of engineering spend is crucial to retain their reputation for a well maintained fleet. It is also important that they maintain an efficient website and online booking process through IT investment otherwise they may incur additional costs elsewhere to rectify problems. Flyjet uses Zero Based Budgeting to achieve cost reductions.

- Flyjet operate a complicated pricing structure which relies on adequate and timely information.

Reference material 3 – Fleet information

- The Flyjet fleet is kept simple to reduce the costs of maintenance and training.

- Potential to switch suppliers to new type of aircraft. Operating costs are lower than current aircraft but retraining of pilots, crew and maintenance staff needs to be considered.

Reference material 4 – Share price information

- Flyjet's share price has remained relatively flat for several years. Investors will be looking for ways to achieve better growth.

- National Air's share price peaked in March 2014 following a period of growth and has started to decline slightly.

Reference material 5 – Summary of company directors

- The Board of Flyjet are experienced albeit relatively old. There is an equal balance of executive and non-executive directors.

- IT and Engineering are not represented at board level.

Reference material 6 – Risk assessment

- According to the risk assessment the only risk which has increased since previous periods is the reliance on IT systems. This needs to be considered alongside the fact that there is currently no IT director on the Board.

- Flyjet invests in maintenance and engineering as well as training in order to mitigate many of the risks it faces.

- Risks involving the economic environment and competition are less controllable and present significant challenges to Flyjet.

Reference material 7 – Corporate social responsibility information

- Flyjet has a CSR policy focused on its relationship with the key stakeholders of customers, staff and the environment. These three key areas seem to be reflected in the investments made by the company in engineering and training.

- Staff are a key stakeholder and appear to be unionised so could be quite disruptive. Redundancies have already been made so employees are likely to be feeling vulnerable and this may affect staff loyalty and therefore turnover.

- There is no mention of how Flyjet intends to treat suppliers and this could be considered a weakness.

Reference material 8 – Financial statement extracts

Ratio analysis was performed in Chapter Five and the results are shown here:

Ratio	2015	2014
Revenue growth	11%	–
Operating profit margin	(3%)	1%
Return on Capital Employed (ROCE)	(3.8%)	0.8%
Current ratio	1.17:1	1.49:1
Receivables days	18 days	21 days
Inventory days	4 days	4 days
Payables days	44 days	47 days
Gearing	25%	44%

Commentary:

- Flyjet has achieved revenue growth but is under pressure in terms of profit margin.

- The working capital position is broadly the same as the previous year although arguably an improvement to reduce receivables days and payables days to manage the relationship with suppliers.

- Higher overall payables and a reduced cash balance has impacted the current ratio and this needs careful monitoring in the short term.

- The level of debt has reduced significantly which has had a positive effect on gearing. This presents the possibility of further debt finance being raised in the future.

Reference material 9 – Financial statement extracts for another airline

Extending the analysis above yields the following:

Ratio	Flyjet 2015	National Air 2015
Revenue growth	11%	15%
Operating profit margin	(3%)	9.5%
Return on Capital Employed (ROCE)	(3.8%)	0.8%
Current ratio	1.17:1	1.33:1
Receivables days	18 days	6 days
Inventory days	4 days	1.2 days
Payables days	44 days	9 days
Gearing	25%	70%

National Air seems to be a much stronger position financially compared with Flyjet.

- As well as showing an increase in revenue they are also maintaining a positive operating profit margin which is consistent with the prior year.

- This is in spite of the cost analysis in exhibit 2 showing they have a much higher cost per available seat kilometre.

- National Air is a full service airline and therefore are clearly charging a premium price for this differentiated service.

- Short term liquidity for National Air does not appear to be an issue but the level of debt is high which may limit future growth.

3 SWOT analysis

A SWOT analysis is a useful tool to summarise the current position of the company. It is simply a listing of the following:

- The STRENGTHS of the organisation. These are internal factors that give the organisation a distinct advantage.

- The WEAKNESSES of the organisation. These are internal factors that affect performance adversely, and so might put the organisation at a disadvantage.

- The OPPORTUNITIES available. These are circumstances or developments in the environment that the organisation might be in a position to exploit to its advantage.

- The THREATS or potential threats. These are factors in the environment that present risks or potential risks to the organisation and its competitive position.

Strengths and weaknesses are internal to the organisation, whereas opportunities and threats are external factors.

A SWOT analysis can be presented simply as a list of strengths, followed by weaknesses, then opportunities and finally threats. It would be useful to indicate within each category which factors seem more significant than others, perhaps by listing them in descending order of priority. Alternatively a SWOT analysis, if it is not too long and excludes minor factors, can be presented in the form of a 2 × 2 table, as follows:

Strengths	Weaknesses
Opportunities	Threats

With this method of presentation, the positive factors (strengths and opportunities) are listed on the left and the negative factors (weaknesses and threats) are on the right.

Test your understanding 1

Prepare a SWOT analysis of Flyjet based on the summary of each exhibit and the guidance above.

Strengths	Weaknesses
Opportunities	**Threats**

4 Summary

You should now be comfortable with all the key issues identified in the Flyjet pre-seen and ready to start thinking about the exam.

Next steps:

(1) It is a good idea, once you have analysed the pre-seen, to brainstorm a list of possible triggers (what might happen) and tasks (what you have to do) which you may face in the exam.

This is NOT an exercise in question spotting as you cannot hope to simply guess the requirements and only study a limited amount of topics. However this brainstorm will help you to think about how the pre-seen may relate to the competencies and may mean fewer complete surprises on the day of the exam.

Warning: In the past some candidates seem to have been a little guilty of drafting "pre-fabricated" answers based on pre-seen material and then simply writing these out in the exam. It is vital that you address the new information in the unseen material and reflect the specifics of the requirements.

Test your understanding answers

Test your understanding 1

Strengths	Weaknesses
• Reputation for safety • Relatively low cost base • Experienced board • Low gearing • Maximised seat capacity • Some good areas of social responsibility	• Loss making • Simplified fleet leading to deskilled workforce • Stagnant share price • No reference to suppliers in CSR policy • Lack of IT and Engineering representation at board level
Opportunities	**Threats**
• Further reductions in costs e.g fuel • Offer greater level of service to compete with companies such as National Air • Acquisition of competitor • New routes • Additional products such as car hire and hotels • Opportunity to switch aircraft suppliers	• Prices undercut by competition • Increase in wealth may reduce demand for no-frills • Increases in fuel prices • Further recession/depression reducing demand for all travel • Terrorist threat or safety incident affecting reputation • Disruption caused by supplier unable/unwilling to continue to trade with Flyjet • Strike action

7

Practice triggers and tasks

Chapter learning objectives

- To understand how underlying knowledge from E2, P2 and F2 could be applied within the case study

1 Introduction

In previous chapters you have been introduced to the concept of triggers and tasks and in Chapter Six we have helped you to prepare and analyse the pre-seen information for the pilot exam – Flyjet. Before we think about the exam day itself we will do some practice exercises which will help you prepare for as many different scenarios as possible arising in the exam. This will also give you an opportunity to revise some key aspects of the syllabus and consider how they may be applied to the scenario. It is crucial that you go through this process to fully prepare yourself for the exam.

However, you need to be careful – this is NOT an exercise in question spotting. We are aiming to revise the knowledge required and practise the skills needed to perform well in any exam rather than guess what may come up. Any set of pre-seen exhibits can give rise to a huge range of possible tasks – we have only provided a sample here.

Once you understand the competencies by which this exam will be marked, are completely comfortable with the syllabus diagnostics at the beginning of Chapter Three and have thoroughly prepared the pre-seen information produced in Chapter Four then you are ready to continue with these exercises. Each task begins with a small scenario (or trigger) to introduce the topic and set the scene. You should be using the skills discussed in Chapter Eight to work through these tasks. These tasks are discrete – i.e. they do not follow on from each other but stand alone as sample exercises. Later on in this book we will consider how the tasks will flow into a complete exam.

Note: These task exercises are not related to each other. All you need to attempt this task is the pre-seen material and the additional material provided below. You should not make reference to any material provided for other practice tasks.

2 E2 – Project and relationship management

Exercise – 1

Recent events in Flyjet's home country:

National Air has recently issued a press release which has resulted in an increase in their share price over the last few weeks. The press release focusses on their strong safety record, high customer satisfaction ratings where customers are stated as having said 'we always feel we're in safe hands with National Air and their attentive staff' and their efficient IT booking systems. As support to their claims they have provided a breakdown of their 2013 costs, analysed per available seat kilometre.

Details are provided below:

Fuel	1.8
Staff costs	1.7
Engineering	1.4
Depreciation	1.2
Information Technology	1.0
Landing and Airport Parking	1.2
In-flight meals	1.3
TOTAL	9.6

National Air has also stated that their company goes from strength to strength with a 15% increase on profit from prior year.

Simone Connelly recently phoned you with the following information:

Flyjet's shareholders have shown some concern regarding this press release. They have contacted Simone and demanded a response as to whether or not Flyjet lags behind National Air in these areas and why Flyjet is incapable of attaining the standard set by National Air.

The Finance Director has asked you to draft a letter to the shareholders dealing with their concerns. She would like you to concentrate on the relative spend of Flyjet when it comes to staff costs, safety, and IT systems and whether or not they have less commitment to these areas than that demonstrated by National Air.

She would also like you to suggest how Flyjet might alter their inflight meal service to increase margins and whether or not depreciation costs are making overall company comparisons unrealistic.

Exercise – 2

The following e-mail has been sent to Simone Connelly, the Finance Director, from Patrick Dunlop, the HR director:

Re: Staff appraisals

We have recruited a new HR manager from our competitor National Air and I have been discussing with her National Air's approach to the staff appraisal process.

For appraisals, it seems that National Air does things quite differently. The HR department conducts performance reviews of staff centrally only once a year, using a more formal approach of self-appraisal followed by completion of a checklist at the interviews.

Flyjet, as you know, adopts a more informal approach, with each member of staff being given a 'face to face' appraisal by their line manager every quarter. We did once undertake a self-appraisal exercise prior to each meeting, but this was discontinued two years ago in the face of sustained resistance from staff.

This would seem to be a good opportunity to review our staff appraisal process to ensure that it continues to reflect best practice and to meet the ongoing needs of our organisation. I would welcome a meeting to discuss this further.

Kind regards,
Patrick

In response the Finance Director has sent you the following e-mail:

Re: Staff Appraisals

Patrick Dunlop, our HR director, has a requested a meeting to review our staff appraisal process: I attach his e-mail for your information.

As we have recently 'poached' an HR manager from National Air, it would seem too good an opportunity to miss to compare Flyjet's approach to that of our competition.

In preparation for the meeting I would like you to prepare a report for me on the principles of the appraisal process and the key features of the approaches adopted by Flyjet and National Air. In particular, I would like you to consider who should undertake the appraisals, how they should be conducted and their optimum frequency.

Simone Connelly
Finance Director

Exercise – 3

The following e-mail has been sent to Simone Connelly, the Finance Director, from Charles Brown, the Marketing Director:

Hi Simone,

I'm just dashing out to a conference and am in need of a quick favour.

As you know, a new project team has been established to look at the profit margins on the in-flight food and drink sales. The lower profit items may be removed to make way for a new range of products. No firm decisions have been made yet on the new items to be stocked but we're considering teddy bears, perfumes and watches.

Humera from the marketing department has been put in charge of the team which consists of members of marketing, finance and sales. She's never led a team before but is a very capable member of staff and in need of new challenges. She'd just like a few pointers on how to lead and motivate the team. Any chance you could jot down the main areas for her to keep in mind?

All the best,
Charles

In response the Finance Director has sent you the following e-mail:

From: Simone Connelly
Sent: Today, 10.07am

Subject: Leadership summary for Humera

I've attached an email above from Charles Brown. I'd like you to deal with his request as quickly as possible as this project could be vital to the increased profitability of Flyjet going forward.

Please email a report back to me at your earliest convenience.

Regards,
Simone
Finance Director

Exercise – 4

Extract from an article in Travel News Monthly:

Manage those conflicts to maximise profits!

A recent study shows that conflict in project teams if not sorted quickly can easily escalate into full-blown arguments, disrupting the group and stopping work in its tracks. Managers must be on the look-out for resentments seething under the surface, and act quickly to resolve the situation before it gets out of hand.

The Finance Director has sent you the following e-mail:

From: Simone Connelly
Sent: Today

Subject: Managing Team Conflicts

I enclose an article from a recent trade journal which raises some interesting points that could be relevant to Flyjet. I met with the HR Director Patrick Dunlop over lunch the other day and he said there have been recent problems with some members of the flight teams not getting on. It may be helpful to remind our senior flight attendants of the pitfalls of team conflicts and to give them a few ideas on how to deal with them effectively.

With this in mind I would like you to prepare a hand-out that can be used as part of a training exercise for our senior cabin staff. This should address the key principles of dealing effectively with conflict.

Simone Connelly
Finance Director

3 P2 – Advanced management accounting

Exercise – 5

Headlines in a national newspaper read:

National Air Flying High With Industry Award

Top executives at National Air were celebrating after scooping a prestigious award for Best Customer Service at the travel industry awards ceremony last night.

Their Chief Executive commented, 'At National Air we pride ourselves on giving value for money, but we never compromise on service. The best thing about this award is that it is voted for by the passengers themselves and that means so much to us and to our staff who work hard to maintain consistently high standards of customer care. We would like to thank our customers for their loyalty and continued support.'

The Finance Director has sent you the following e-mail:

From: Simone Connelly
Sent: Today

Subject: Balanced Scorecard for Non-Financial Performance Management

The board is setting up a working party to consider ways to respond to our main competitor winning the top award for customer care last week. One of the measures we are thinking of introducing to Flyjet is the 'Balanced Scorecard' ('BSC') approach to non-financial Key Performance Indicators.

I will be delivering a brief talk to introduce the concept to the working party and for that I would like you to prepare a slide with no more than ten bullet points to explain the rationale for the BSC and to give a few examples of measures that Flyjet could use.

The slide should focus on non-financial measures only.

Simone Connelly
Finance Director

Exercise – 6

A member of the aircraft design team has presented two new ideas to the board for their consideration. Both look at increasing capacity of the aircraft in terms of number of seats available.

A junior in the finance department has analysed the options.

Project 1

By removing one toilet from the smaller aircraft it is possible to install an extra row of seats. This work can be done in-house and would be completed in a few months. Current flights would not be affected as the work could be done in aircraft 'downtime'.

- NPV of the project over 5 years = $500m

- Initial investment = $74m

- Payback period = 3.2 years

- ROCE = 26%

Project 2

The seats in all the aircraft could be moved a little closer together. This would allow an extra 2 rows of seats to be installed and does not contravene any legal requirements. Although the installation can be done by the in-house team the actual seats would need to be manufactured externally for Flyjet and the overhaul of the inside of the aeroplanes would take significant time, meaning flight patterns may need to be altered for several months.

- NPV of the project over 8 years = $720m

- Initial investment = $97m

- Payback period = 2.1 years

- ROCE = 23%

Please note: all calculations have been performed using the company's current cost of capital. The project will be funded by debt.

These projects are mutually exclusive. A mixture of both is not considered to be financially viable.

Simone Connelly has sent you the following note:

From: Simone Connelly
Sent: Today

Subject: Project Appraisal

Hi

I've dropped some figures on your desk regarding two projects that Flyjet could undertake.

I'd like a summary of the suitability of the investment appraisal techniques of NPV, payback and ROCE – I'll use it as notes for my next board meeting.

Please also provide a summary of other factors that we should consider before taking on either of these overhauls. I don't require any recalculation of figures.

Simone Connelly
Finance Director

Exercise – 7

Headlines in a national newspaper read::

Baggage Handling Dispute at Dublansk Enters its Second Week

Passengers travelling to and from Dublansk airport face continued delays to flights and long queues in the baggage reclaim hall as unions strike over cuts to their hours. Airhold, who operate the baggage handling service, said as discussions were ongoing, it would be inappropriate to comment.

The following month you receive an email from Simone Connelly, the Finance Director, as follows:

From: Simone Connelly
Sent: Today

Subject: Uncontrollable Costs and Performance Management

I have received a call from a senior manager in HR asking for advice in dealing with a staff matter.

A very disgruntled Operations Manager from Dublansk airport has had their promotion put back after results of the airport division were badly affected by the costs of the baggage handling dispute last month. The baggage handlers are not directly employed by Flyjet, but the delays in the loading and unloading of luggage resulted in a significant cost to this division of Flyjet from aircraft missing their allotted take-off and landing 'slots'.

The airport manager is complaining that he should not be penalised for costs that were not within his control.

I would like you to prepare notes for my meeting with the HR manager tomorrow to discuss the matter. The notes should focus on the distinction between controllable and uncontrollable costs and the implications of this for performance management.

Simone Connelly
Finance Director

Exercise – 8

The following extract appeared in this morning's national newspaper:

Funigua Volcano Shows Increased Activity

Western Europe's most active volcano has shown heightened activity in recent weeks. Seismologists who had declared the volcano dormant until 1998 registered 30 explosions on Monday. Although the activity lessened again overnight, a full scale eruption has not yet been ruled out. An ash cloud up to 2km in height has been seen rising from the volcano over the past few days.

You have received the following email from Simone Connelly, the Finance Director:

From: Simone Connelly
Sent: Today

Subject: Risk management

Good morning.

I've just received a call from Aileen Adams who has scheduled an emergency meeting for this afternoon. She saw the front cover of this morning's paper and the increased threat of volcanic eruption and has thus brought forward our risk management review.

Could you please prepare me 2 slides to incorporate into my presentation for the board?

I would like the first slide to provide an overview of the risk management process and to select a suitable framework for risk management that Flyjet might adopt.

The second slide should explain the structure of this framework and give specific examples of risks faced by Flyjet and how they can be or have been managed.

I'll be at my desk until 11am so please email me before then.

Simone Connelly
Finance Director

---

4 F2 – Advanced financial accounting

Exercise – 9

New appointment at board level

Flyjet has recently recruited a new IT director to sit on the board. He has come from another airline company operating a similar 'no frills' policy to Flyjet, but he considers his previous company to have a much stronger IT system in place.

The new director wishes the board to invest in a system upgrade which is expected to significantly reduce the IT threat to the company for the next eight years.

You have received the following request from Simone Connelly:

I have recently reviewed the IT director's suggestion of an IT system upgrade for Flyjet. It looks like a financially viable solution with a strong NPV based on Flyjet's current cost of capital. However, significant finance would be needed to get this project off the ground.

I need a presentation for the board discussing the pros and cons of different sources of long term finance. I'd like you to provide me with a broad overview of debt versus equity in a two slide presentation, with a maximum of 5 bullet points on each topic.

Kind regards,
Simone

Exercise – 10

Flyjet has issued the following press release:

Flyjet is pleased to announce a new joint venture with Airlo, Caprese Airlines and Hofliegen to 'air share' on a number of Western European flight routes.

A memorandum of understanding has been signed, and the deal will dramatically expand Flyjet's European route network, improving connections and onward transfer flights for our customers.

You have received the following e-mail from Simone Connelly, the Finance Director:

From: Simone Connelly
Sent: Today

Subject: IFRS Implications of Joint Venture

You will have seen the press release on the proposed joint venture to passenger-share with three other European airlines.

The accounting treatment of this arrangement could be complex, particularly regarding the provisions of IFRS 12. The treatment will depend on the precise terms of the contract and this is not finalised; only the 'Heads of Agreement' have been signed. Nevertheless, I raised the matter of IFRS 12 at the board meeting last week and not surprisingly most of my colleagues had little, if any, knowledge of it.

Before the next board meeting tomorrow I would like you to draft an explanatory note on the rationale for IFRS 12, explaining WHY interests in other entities should be disclosed.

This is to be a brief memorandum only. Explanation of the likely treatment of the joint venture in our accounts or indeed, a draft disclosure note is NOT required at this stage.

Simone Connelly
Finance Director

Exercise – 11

Dismissal

A member of the management accounting team has recently been dismissed from Flyjet following a series of verbal and written warnings.

There have been problems with this member of staff for some time of which the board are fully aware. He sent the following email just before his dismissal to a number of members in the finance team. The IT department recovered the contents of the email from the server – an extract of which is shown below.

From: Gary Robinson
To: Adil, Clare, Mark

...If I was you, I'd be stripping out those depreciation figures to make our ROCE look better. After all, depreciation isn't a real number anyway – it's just guess work. What other hope have we of getting a bonus this year?   I heard the guys at National Air are in for a massive profit based bonus. They have all the luck! ...

You have received the following communication from Simone Connelly:

From: Simone Connelly
Sent: Today

Subject: Ethics and accounting policies

An alarming email was sent by Gary around some of the accounts team just before his dismissal. This email is attached for your information. I've since spoken to everyone that received the email and they are appalled by its content and Gary's inappropriate suggestions.

Whilst I'm certain that no one in our finance department is in any way considering these unethical suggestions I'd like to send a memo round to all members of the accounts team reminding them of a few key ideas.

Could you please draft some notes that I can include, briefly covering Agency Theory and why it is unethical to manipulate accounting policies and estimates for our own gain?

I'd also like notes on areas where Flyjet's policies could come under scrutiny. Please concentrate on depreciation and amortisation, and those items included in operating expenses.

Simone Connelly
Finance Director

Exercise – 12

This report has appeared in the business press:

Flyjet snaps up Aerdrago

Flyjet, the low-cost airline, has acquired the 'lion's share of troubled European carrier Aerdrago, in a multi-million Euro move that has taken the markets by surprise. The news has been received well by analysts, with Flyjet's share price jumping by 14 cents following the announcement. Travel industry analyst Bill Holmes commented, 'This is a bold move by Flyjet and could work well for them, bolstering their routes in Europe. Rumours are rife that they got Aerdrago at a bargain price.'

The following note has been left on your desk by Simone Connelly, the Finance Director:

I attach a press report on our purchase of the Eastern European carrier Aerdrago for your information. This raises accounting issues for our department.

I know you have already prepared the material for your talk to the trainees on 'Accounting for Subsidiaries' later this week, but I think something brief on the accounting implications of acquiring a foreign subsidiary under the provisions of IAS21 should be added.

A summary sheet covering how to translate the results of a foreign subsidiary for consolidation would be suitable.

Perhaps you can let me have this by the end of the day.

Thanks,
Simone

---

5 Summary

You should better understand the wide range of possible tasks which you may encounter in the exam. You should also have a better appreciation of the level of detail required in your answers to score a high mark in the exam.

Next steps:

(1) Have you attempted all of the tasks in this chapter? Don't be tempted to look at the answers until you have, at the very least, made detailed notes on your response.

(2) If you struggled with any of these tasks, this may indicate a knowledge gap which you need to revisit.

Test your understanding answers

Exercise – 1

Note: These suggested answers are indicative of what could be produced by a very competent student, in the time allowed, and would earn a good pass. They are not 'reference', or 'model', answers. Other, equally valid, points would receive credit. It is important that you attempt to produce your own answers and then reflect on whether you have addressed the requirement BEFORE reviewing these suggested solutions.

Dear Shareholders,

Following the recent press release by National Air and their increased share price, I am writing to respond to the analysis of their cost breakdown and the statements made regarding the quality of service, standard of safety and IT system reliability offered by National Air in comparison to Flyjet.

Flyjet have always applied a strong policy of Corporate Social Responsibility, whereby we not only care for the environment in which we operate with reduced emission aircraft and low levels of noise pollution, but also for the wellbeing and competence of our staff in their working life.

Following the recent redundancy programme, Flyjet is a leaner, more efficient organisation. Increased staff morale from ongoing job security is resulting in enhanced customer satisfaction and improved reputation for Flyjet. National Air's staff costs, whilst higher than Flyjet's per available seat kilometre (ASK), actually result in the same percentage of overall cost (17.7%), and Flyjet's commitment to staff training has resulted in an overall increase in staff costs from 2014 to 2015, demonstrating our continued commitment to safety and customer satisfaction.

As a no frills airline it is our policy to keep costs down by charging for inflight meals and minimising landing and airport parking charges, but safety is always our primary concern and our training programme is recognised as one of the best in the industry, with a company culture firmly focussed on risk identification and management.

Engineering costs in 2013 were identical for National Air and Flyjet at 1.4cents per ASK, but again it can be seen that as a percentage of total spend, National Air's engineering only accounts for 14.6% of costs whereas Flyjet spends 20.6% on engineering. Even though we are a much smaller company than National Air, aircraft servicing and maintenance is a top priority and we will never compromise customer safety in an effort to reduce cost. Our company has an excellent reputation with respect to safety and the high utilisation rate of our aircraft (86% compared to National Air's 75%) shows the utmost confidence of our passengers.

With regard to the IT systems employed by Flyjet, 13.2% of our ASK cost in 2013 was for IT spend compared to 10.4% for National Air. Flyjet has rationalised the booking systems with the removal of call centres, in recognition of today's widespread access to the internet and, as such, it is strongly focussed on the quality of these systems, ensuring spending keeps our facilities up to date for all user needs.

From the costing information provided by National Air, almost 14% of their ASK costs relate to inflight meals. By contrast, Flyjet make profit from meals and snacks sold as part of the on-board offerings available to customers. Research into the margins of these products is to be carried out to identify potential cost savings. It may be possible to streamline the offerings made, concentrating on a smaller range of products which are more popular with customers or to renegotiate the current range for a better deal from the suppliers. This will all help to ensure growth of Flyjet's profits going forward whilst not reducing our reputation in key areas such as safety.

It should also be noted that whilst National Air quote a 15% increase on prior year profit figures, no depreciation of their fleet has been charged in recent years. Removing the $726m depreciation charge from Flyjet's 2015 accounts results in a profit of $660m and as such, provides a better comparison with National Air's position. Our depreciation policy is based on historic costs of aircraft and their useful lives and we keep this policy consistent to promote truth, fairness and comparability for our account users.

We hope that the above information is of use to you in regards to National Air's press release. Should you have any further queries which you would like to discuss, please do not hesitate to get in touch.

Yours faithfully,
Simone Connelly

Exercise – 2

Report on the Flyjet Appraisal Process

Performance appraisal is a process of formal communication between employee and management, designed to identify the strengths and weaknesses in a member of staff, to assess their potential for promotion and to devise objectives for training and development. It is an important component of the proper management of staff, to recognise contribution and to enhance commitment to the company and its goals.

A number of approaches can be adopted, but in general appraisals should be open and constructive in style, present a balanced view, and should give both parties an opportunity to air any matters of concern. They are usually based on past performance but may also project forward to incorporate future development and training needs.

Who undertakes the Appraisal?

In National Air, the HR department undertakes all appraisals. This has the advantage of being objective, but is impersonal and has been described by theorists as being something of a 'last resort'. Flyjet by comparison relies on an immediate line manager, on the basis that they are best placed to judge the performance of their staff. Provided our managers are well-trained and aware of the need for objectivity, appraisal by an immediate superior should work well, so on this basis it is recommended that Flyjet's current practice is retained.

Methodology

There are a variety of approaches to appraisal, but at present Flyjet relies on regular but relatively informal discussions or 'chats', with a note being taken of salient points by the manager for inclusion in the employee's staff file, whereas it appears that National Air uses a checklist as a basis for appraisal interviews. This is perhaps something Flyjet should consider adopting as a more comprehensive and standardised approach.

Checklists can be adapted to suit each category of staff, with those for service-based roles such as cabin crew focussing on aspects of performance based on customer service and those for engineering staff focussing on technical skills. It is proposed that the staff member and manager go through this together at each appraisal meeting and use it as a basis for discussion, with the completed checklist acting as a formal record of the review process.

As a starting-point for the appraisal process organisations can also use self-appraisal techniques to supplement input from the direct line manager. Flyjet did employ this technique, requiring completion of a form by the employee prior to the 'face to face' interview, but this was abandoned two years ago as staff strongly resisted being obliged to rate their own performance. Whilst self-assessment may have focussed the employees' minds on their performance over the review period, the responses received were thought to be so subjective that little useful information was gleaned and the process seemed counter-productive. Removing this stage has simplified the appraisal process for Flyjet, saving time and reducing costs.

Frequency of Appraisal

Flyjet's present system of quarterly appraisal is labour-intensive and is arguably too frequent: it risks interfering with the company's operations and allowing insufficient time for an individual to respond to points made at an appraisal before the next is upon them. If a more formalised 'checklist' approach is adopted, this could be an opportunity to spread reviews out. The annual review system of National Air on the other hand is open to the criticism that by the time appraisals do take place they may be so out of date as to have little relevance. With this in mind, a twice-yearly appraisal could perhaps be explored as a good compromise. This should allow management to ensure staff are meeting objectives and equally should allow staff to raise concerns on a timely basis.

To summarise, the present system of review by an immediate superior works well and should be retained, but a more formal, objective checklist approach may be beneficial on a six-monthly basis.

I hope this report is helpful. Please contact me if you have any questions.

Exercise – 3

To: Simone Connelly
From: Management Accountant
Date: Today

Subject: Team leadership and motivation

Please find below a summary of team leadership responsibilities and how to motivate a new project team with regards to the sale of in-flight products.

How to lead a new project team

It is often stated that there is no 'correct' way to lead a team and that styles change according to the circumstances of a project and the team members' needs. Whilst it is the leader's responsibility to provide direction they do not necessarily always need definite answers at the start of a project, but rather a balanced concern for the task in hand and the people conducting the work.

Successful completion of a project can be achieved by considering group needs, task needs and individual needs.

Group needs

This group has already been established, so it is now the leader's responsibility to ensure regular communication takes place, encouraging team building and trust between members. Discipline must also be provided to promote goal congruence and motivation should be given to ensure members achieve results.

Task needs – discipline

This can be broadly divided into setting objectives, planning tasks, allocating responsibilities and setting performance standards.

In this particular project, competitor analysis could be undertaken to see what products other airlines offer and at what price. Flyjet currently makes 0.2 cents per available seat kilometre on food and drinks but with higher margin products a new target could be set.

As a 'no frills' airline the quality of products should also be considered. Sales staff could examine the range of jewellery and perfumes offered by competitors and their appeal to Flyjet's customer demographic. The finance staff could then assess margins to help the team consider whether or not inclusion in Flyjet's range will be suitable.

Marketing team members could be tasked with new ways to promote product sales. For instance, competitor airlines hold competitions for their branded teddy bears being photographed 'on holiday' and this gives customers a chance to win a free flight on the network.

Individual needs – motivation

Motivation of an individual can be described as their willingness to perform a task and dedication to the achievement of goals. A team leader should coach their staff, providing fresh challenges, then recognising and praising achievement of tasks.

Given that the current team has been formed from existing Flyjet employees it is likely that basic needs of salary and job security have already been satisfied, so the team leader should look at higher levels of motivation. These can be classed as 'social', 'ego' and 'self-fulfilment' needs.

Social needs such as ensuring a good working relationship can be fostered by regular meetings and open communication. To satisfy ego needs, the team leader might discuss with the board whether or not bonuses will be available for a successful project outcome. A new job title could also be given for the duration of the project and success on this task could lead to inclusion on future Flyjet teams who examine long term growth of the business, offering the team members new challenges and opportunities for career advancement.

I hope this summary is of some help in the initialisation of the in-flight product range group and should you need any more detail on leadership and motivation techniques, please let me know.

Exercise – 4

Resolving Conflict in Teams

When people come together to work in a team they bring strengths from a diversity of approaches which can lead to increased efficiency and synergy for the group, but this also means that an element of conflict is, to some extent, inevitable. Conflict arises from differences between people, in terms of power, of values and of attitudes, but it need not be a wholly destructive force.

If it is identified quickly and handled properly, conflict can result in more open communication and improved creativity, and lead to renewed commitment by team members to the task in hand. The key principle to bear in mind is that differences in viewpoint should be resolved quickly, before they escalate into full-scale disputes. Studies show that many managers prefer to ignore conflicts, and that they simply may not be giving them the attention they deserve.

Sources of Conflict

Conflict arises from many sources; from poor communication, from structural issues and from personal problems. To apply this to a cabin crew situation, communication conflicts could arise from poor listening skills, lack of shared information such as flight delays or problems with a passenger. 'Structural' conflict in this context would include disputes over the extent to which someone is a 'team player', resentment over different pay scales or rank and personal conflict might arise from a flight attendant's self-esteem issues or problems at home. Senior cabin staff need to be aware of these potential sources of conflict in their team and to react swiftly to problems to 'nip them in the bud'.

Resolving the Conflict

The following stages are useful:

(1) Acknowledge the conflict. Bring the issue out into the open, discussing the impact on performance with the team and to agree to a process of trying to resolve the issue. 'Active listening' is a key skill here, being ready to understand and empathise with another person's point of view.

(2) Understand the Situation. A team leader should take time to ensure each person's view is heard and to understand that point of view; it may be necessary to see through strong emotions and it is always advisable to remain objective and to stop issues from becoming personal. Breaking the team into smaller groups to air a matter can work well and can prevent cabin crew team members from 'ganging up' on each other.

(3) Reach Agreement. The team leader should reconvene and bring the team back together to agree what needs to be done to overcome the conflict. Compromise may be necessary, which could leave each side feeling dissatisfied or, if handled well, can enhance unity in the team with both sides feeling that they have made a positive contribution by 'giving up' something to make the team work.

Key points to Remember

Senior staff should always try to prevent conflict in their teams where possible, and it may be worth bearing these principles in mind:

- Develop clear communication in the team;

- Focus only on 'actionable' solutions e.g. if a flight is delayed, that cannot be changed, but how the cabin crew responds to and deals with the situation can be managed;

- Avoid allocating blame; remain positive and allow team members to 'save face';

- Maintain respect for each other at all times.

Conflict is an on-going issue for leaders of a team to deal with, but if tackled promptly can often be readily resolved.

Exercise – 5

The Balanced Scorecard: Non-financial Indicators for Performance Management

Context

- In today's market it is no longer enough to focus solely on profit. Customers expect an 'all-round package' of value combined with service, and as a company we must respond to these demands to maintain a competitive edge.

- Aside from financial aspects Flyjet should consider the 'Customer Perspective', the 'Internal Perspective' and the 'Innovation and Learning Perspective', identifying a series of goals measured by key performance indicators ('KPI's) consistent with the company's strategic vision.

The Customer Perspective: How do customers see us?

- The Goal: To offer aircraft seats to passengers at the lowest cost.

  The KPI: To benchmark the average price per seat compared to our competitors.

- The Goal: To reduce flight delays to a less than ten minutes on average.

  The KPI: To measure the % of departures within ten minutes of the scheduled time-slot.

The Internal Perspective: What must we excel at?

- The Goal: To maximise employee satisfaction.

  The KPI: Measurement of staff turnover.

- The Goal: To keep IT 'downtime' to a minimum.

  The KPI: Number of IT 'blackouts' per month.

The Innovation and Learning Perspective: Can we continue to improve and add value?

- The Goal: To encourage staff creativity and learning.

  The KPI: The % or number of staff suggestions implemented

- The Goal: To develop the skills of staff.

  The KPI: % of time spent on training.

Exercise – 6

SUMMARY OF INVESTMENT APPRAISAL TECHNIQUES

Flyjet is presented with two mutually exclusive projects which provide an absolute increase in shareholder wealth. The suitability of different appraisal techniques is discussed below, along with other financial and non-financial factors that Flyjet should consider.

NPV

NPV is often regarded as a superior method of investment appraisal. It is a discounted cash flow technique which allows for decline in the real value of money over time due to inflation.

Based on cash flow rather than profit, it is not a subjective method which depends on accounting policies.

It can, however, be considered a complex calculation and a decision needs to be made as to a suitable cost of capital to use as a discount rate.

In this case, project 2 has the higher NPV ($720m v $500m) so would lead to a greater increase in shareholder wealth, suggesting project 2 should be chosen.

However, the life of project 2 is three years longer than project 1 so information is needed on project 1 beyond the 5 year timeframe.

Payback

Payback is a more simplistic technique which is widely understood.

As with NPV, it uses cash flow rather than profit, and favouring quick returns, it can be thought to limit risk. Given that Flyjet has a weak cash position this maximisation of liquidity may be preferable.

However, payback ignores the overall project profitability and does not consider returns after the payback period which could be significant.

Project 2 has a shorter payback period (2.1 years v 3.2 years) but a larger initial investment is required and the willingness of banks to lend this money must be considered.

ROCE

ROCE is also considered to be a relatively simple technique and quick to calculate but it does not account for the project life or the timing of cash flows.

It also gives no consideration of the absolute gain and is dependent on accounting policies as it uses profit in the calculation.

Project 2 has a lower ROCE than project 1 (23% v 26%) suggesting that project 1 should be chosen in preference – but Flyjet would have to decide a target ROCE that makes projects acceptable to the company and whether either project meets this target. This makes ROCE subjective and use of profit can leave it open to manipulation.

Other factors to consider

Using the current cost of capital for calculations may not be appropriate as the projects affect the gearing of the company. Project 1 ($74m investment) will increase Flyjet's gearing from 25% to 29%, and project 2 ($97m investment) results in a gearing of 30%. Cost of capital may need to be adjusted for differing levels of risk.

Project lives are also not comparable. Project 2 over eight years is a longer term investment, making cash flows more difficult to predict with accuracy. This is especially true given the volatility of the airline industry during a time of recession.

Customer comfort must also be considered. Flyjet already has one fewer toilet per aircraft than National Air. This, coupled with reduced legroom in project 2 could lead to passenger discomfort and may result in travellers choosing not to use Flyjet. A loss of passengers will affect revenue figures used in the NPV calculations and the current 86% utilisation rate may reduce further. Project 2 also causes temporary disruption to flight patterns which may result in passengers choosing to fly with competitors.

However, more seats could allow a reduction in ticket price, increasing market share. Flyjet would have to balance whether cheaper seats are more valued by customers than on-board comfort and whether either of these projects would result in long term growth and stability for Flyjet.

Exercise – 7

Notes for Meeting on Controllable and Uncontrollable Costs in Performance Management

A key issue for companies assessing the performance of their staff is whether they should be held accountable for costs which cannot be influenced by their actions; in other words, that are outside their control. An example of this would be the costs associated with loss of flight 'slots' at an airport or division during a strike, as happened recently at Dublansk.

Theories advocate that on principle, the performance of a divisional manager should only be based on factors within their control, the 'Controllability Principle'. This necessitates separating the economic results of a division from the performance of its manager for the purposes of staff evaluation, including all costs for the division for financial judgements, but excluding non-controllable costs such as foreign exchange losses or centralised administrative charges.

The rationale for focussing only on controllable costs for performance measurement is that if uncontrollable costs are not excluded, sub-optimal management decisions are encouraged. For instance, investment projects may be wrongly rejected on the basis that the Return on Investment ('ROI') may be lower than the existing ROI of the division. Staff may also become demotivated or demoralised by failing to meet prescribed targets, thereby losing a bonus or missing out on promotion. This can have a negative impact on staff morale for the division as a whole.

This issue has led to the development of other measures to assess divisional managers including concepts of 'economic value added' to the business, based on adjusted Residual Income, and the 'Balanced Scorecard' approach, which uses a mixture of financial and non-financial indicators. Curiously, studies have shown that reliance on non-financial performance measures causes the highest levels of dis-satisfaction amongst managers, perhaps attributable to clashes over elements of judgement or subjectivity in the setting of standards or through confusion over trying to attain two sets of targets, financial and non-financial.

Focussing on an element of non-controllable costs can in some respects be beneficial. Managers know these costs must be covered, it puts pressure on other staff around them to cover the costs and it forces the manager to take an interest in the cost of resources that are shared.

Where performance standards are set and variances are analysed, managers can be evaluated by comparing actual with budgeted costs. Alternatively, the starting point can be financial results from which non-controllable costs, such as for lost flight 'slots' in this case, are excluded.

Sometimes, organisations measure performance by partially applying the controllability principle; budgeted costs rather than actual costs are used, so the manager is not held accountable for the variance. This could be used in Flyjet's case. If the strike was not anticipated and budgeted for, the results for that airport division could be compared to the pre-strike budget figures, so the manager would not be held responsible and could still be given credit for aspects of results that were within his control. This would seem a sensible compromise and could be a means of resolving the problem of de-motivation of the staff and management at Dublansk.

I hope this is of assistance. If you have any questions, please let me know.

Exercise – 8

SLIDE 1

Management of an organisation are responsible for establishing a risk management system. The ability of an organisation to identify and manage risks is paramount to its long term survival. Effective risk management is seen as a way of enhancing shareholder value by improving performance.

The process of risk management

This can be explained as:

- Risk identification: risks must be identified by a company before they can be managed

- Risk assessment: this looks at the likelihood of a risk occurring and the impact this risk will have on the company

- Risk planning: involves establishing appropriate risk management policies

- Risk monitoring: examining risks on an ongoing basis to see if they have changed or if new risks have arisen that need to be managed.

Appropriate framework for Flyjet:

T.A.R.A. is a risk management framework that can be used by organisations. Once risks have been identified and assessed they can then be Transferred, Avoided, Reduced or Accepted.

SLIDE 2

TARA applied to Flyjet

- *Transfer* – risks of high impact but low likelihood should be transferred. This can be wholly or in part to a third party e.g. by taking out insurance.

  In the case of Flyjet, insurance could be taken out to cover the costs of accommodation for passengers stranded due to volcanic activity.

- *Avoid* – risks of high impact and high likelihood should be avoided. However, since certain risks can only be avoided by withdrawing from a venture altogether, it is often not practical for a business to take this course.

  In the case of Flyjet, revenues may fall due to the economic recession and whilst we may try to minimise this risk, it cannot be avoided.

- *Reduce* – risks of low impact but high likelihood should be reduced. This could involve implementing controls to reduce the impact of the risk should it occur.

  In the case of Flyjet, a recent increase has been seen in IT systems risk. This risk has been reduced by introducing a full suite of security and backup systems to prevent loss of systems or data.

- *Accept* – risks of low impact and low likelihood will cause little damage to a business and can be accepted.

  In the case of Flyjet, the risk of a passenger contracting food poisoning from a pre-packaged snack is low and if an isolated event, is likely to be a minor incident. Flyjet may therefore choose to accept the risk.

Exercise – 9

PRESENTATION TO THE BOARD

Long term sources of finance – debt versus equity

SLIDE ONE – DEBT

- Flyjet has $1.4bn of property, plant and equipment on the balance sheet against which debt could be secured

- Gearing was reduced from 47% in 2014 to 25% in 2015, and is much lower than National Air's gearing of 70%, meaning that Flyjet is likely to be able to obtain debt finance

- However, increased debt finance will lead to an increased cost of capital for the company, which can reduce the calculated NPV

- Despite the tax shield available for debt finance, ongoing interest payments will have to be met and long term, the amount must be paid back

- As a loss making company with low cash reserves, shareholders may question our ability to meet these repayments, therefore demanding a higher return for their investment, which could lead to a fall in share price

SLIDE TWO – EQUITY

- No repayment of equity funding is required

- Dividend payments are not legally required and no payments are currently made, so investors may not demand them in the near future

- However, with Flyjet's currently low and stagnant share price, it is questionable as to whether a share issue would be fully subscribed

- If current shareholders do not wish to take up a rights issue there could be dilution of control

- A public share issue can be very costly and brings with it the dilemma of how to choose a suitable issue price

Exercise – 10

Accounting Disclosures of Interests in other Entities – An Overview of IFRS 12

Background

The global financial crisis of 2007 and the failure of companies such as Enron focused world attention on the failure of published accounts to adequately reflect risk. The crisis highlighted gaps in the amount of information companies provided to enable shareholders, investors and other users of their financial statements to assess the risks inherent in their company being involved with other organisations.

The International Accounting Standards Board ('IASB') recognised that disclosure requirements under several existing standards, notably IAS 27 on Consolidated Financial Statements, IAS 28 on Interests in Associates and IAS 31 on Interests in Joint Ventures covered a lot of common ground, so IFRS 12 was developed as a new standard, effective from 1 January 2013, to impose additional mandatory disclosures on reporting entities.

Objectives

IFRS 12 sets out various 'disclosure objectives', which for example should allow the users of financial statements to:

- understand significant judgements and assessments to determine the nature of an interest in another entity;

- evaluate the nature and extent of restrictions on the ability to use assets or to settle liabilities of the group; and

- evaluate the nature of change in risk associated with interests.

Impact

The disclosure requirements of IFRS 12 itself are complicated, and require an element of judgement on the part of the preparers of financial statements. For example, details may need to be provided on assets employed or liabilities incurred for joint operations, if this is relevant to the understanding of the financial statements.

For Flyjet, the new joint venture with our European partners will necessitate consideration of the IFRS 12 provisions.

Exercise – 11

Agency Theory and Conflict of Interest

As suggested by agency theory there is often separation between ownership of a company (shareholders) and control of a company (directors). This can lead to a conflict of interest whereby accounting policies and estimates are open to subjectivity, bias and inaccuracy in order to falsely boost or suppress reported profits, which may personally benefit directors and staff.

Ethical problems arising

Users of a company's financial statements rely on these accounts for decision making. It is therefore imperative that the accounts present a true and fair view of the company's performance and position to allow comparison with prior periods and with competitors.

Manipulation of accounts in order to mislead users is against the principles of the financial reporting framework whereby accountants are required to report information fairly, objectively and honestly. Reports should not be incomplete by omission, provided recklessly, materially false or contain misleading statements. The suggestion by the management accountant to remove depreciation from our fleet in order to make our ROCE more comparable to National Air is therefore entirely inappropriate.

Situations specific to Flyjet

Depreciation and amortisation

Flyjet depreciates aircraft based on their historical cost and useful economic life. Whilst it is important that a consistent policy is applied, the development of the new aircraft models which are currently under design may lead to our existing aircraft losing value in terms of resale, and a change in depreciation policy may be required.

Amortisation of landing slots is another subjective area which must be considered. The appropriateness of Flyjet's policy for each airport should be regularly reviewed as the value of landing slots can change dramatically over a short period of time. Flyjet's recent withdrawal from West Airport necessitated a write off of $24m compensation for cancellation of contractual commitments, and the continuing recession in the Eurozone risks a further decrease in demand for air travel.

Other operating expenses

In both 2014 and 2015 Flyjet has experienced losses on disposal – $37m on tangible assets in 2014, $48m on tangible and $2m on intangible in 2015. This may again suggest that the current depreciation policy is not appropriate and that the carrying value of assets in the fleet may need to be reviewed.

Operating lease charges on aircraft have increased by 900% from 2014 to 2015. Whilst there may be a perfectly reasonable explanation for this, it is advisable that the classification of these leases is reviewed to ensure they meet the definition of an operating lease rather than a finance lease. Off balance sheet funding is often viewed as an area of manipulation and correct classification of assets must be ensured.

Shareholders are the legal owners of a company and therefore entitled to sufficient information to enable them to make investment decisions. The more transparent the activities of Flyjet, the more assurance we can offer our stakeholders.

Exercise – 12

Accounting for the results of foreign subsidiaries

Entities in which we have a controlling interest will be consolidated into Flyjet's group accounts at the year end. Where a subsidiary is in a foreign country and where its transactions are recorded in a different currency, we then have to consider how to translate the results of that entity.

IAS 21, effective from 1 January 2012, prescribes how to include foreign operations in the financial statements of an entity such as Flyjet and how to translate the financial statements of the overseas subsidiary into the 'presentation currency' used by Flyjet in its consolidated accounts.

Two main issues arise:

- which exchange rates to use, and
- how to report the effects of changes in exchange rates in the financial statements.

Under the provisions of IAS 21, where an organisation has foreign operations:

- the balance sheet is translated using the closing rate (i.e. at the reporting date);

- the profit and loss account of the foreign entity should be translated at the average rate for the period (the only situation where an average rate is not accepted under IAS 21 is where the currency in question has experienced wide fluctuations in exchange rates during the period for which there are special rules, not covered here); and

- any exchange differences arising on translation between the statement of profit being translated at the average rate and the reserves being translated at the closing rate is included in 'other comprehensive income.'

8

Exam day techniques

Chapter learning objectives

- To develop a carefully planned and thought through strategy to cope with the three hours of exam time

1 Exam Day strategy

Once you have studied the pre-seen, learnt the three subject syllabi thoroughly and practised lots of exercises and mocks, you should be well prepared for the exam.

However, it is still important to have a carefully planned and thought through strategy to cope with those three hours of exam time.

This chapter takes you through some of the key skills to master to ensure all your careful preparation does not go to waste.

2 Importance of time management

Someone once referred to case study exams as "the race against time" and it's difficult to imagine a more accurate description. Being able to do what the examiner is wanting is only half of the battle; being able to deliver it in the time available is another matter altogether. This is even more important than in previous exams you may have faced because each section in the real exam is now timed and that once that time is up you will be moved on. Case study is not like a traditional exam where you can go back to a question if you have extra inspiration or feel you have some time left over. You have to complete each task within the time stated.

For this reason, time management is a key skill required to pass the Case Study Examination.

Successful time management requires two things:

1   A tailored time plan – one that plays to your personal strengths and weaknesses; and
2   Discipline in order to stick to it!

Time robbers

There are a number of ways in which time can be wasted or not used effectively in the Case Study Examination. An awareness of these will help to ensure you don't waste time in your exam.

Inactive reading

The first part of each task must be spent actively reading, processing the information and considering the impact on the organisation, how the issues link together and what could be done to resolve them. You will not have time to have a second detailed read and so these thoughts must be captured first time around.

Too much time spent on presentation

You will be writing your answer in software with some similarities to Microsoft Word however the only functions available are

- Cut
- Copy
- Paste
- Undo
- Redo
- Bold
- Italic
- Underline

The temptation to make various words bold or italics or underlined, is very hard to resist. But, resist you must! There are very few marks available for having a response that is well presented, and these finer details will be worth nothing at all.

Being a perfectionist

Students can often spend such a long time pondering about what to write that over the course of a 3 hour exam, over half of it is spent staring into space.

As you are sitting a computer exam you not only spend time pondering, but also have the ability to delete so can change your mind several times before settling on the right word combinations. Just focus on getting your points down and don't worry about whether they could have been phrased better.

Too much detail on earlier parts of the requirement

As we've said earlier, not finishing answers is a key reason for failing the Case Study Examination. One of the main reasons why students fail to finish a section is a lack of discipline when writing about an issue. They feel they have to get all of their points down rather than selecting the better points and moving on. If a task requires you to discuss three different areas it is vital that you cover all parts adequately.

Too much correction

Often students can re-read paragraphs three or more times before they move on to writing the next part of their answer. Instead, try to leave the read through until the final few minutes of the task and try to correct as many obvious errors as possible. The CIMA marker will be reading and marking your script on screen and it is harder to read and understand the points you are making if there are many typing errors.

3 Assimilation of information

One of the most challenging things to deal with in a case study examination is the volume of information which you have available. This is particularly difficult when you have both pre-seen and unseen information to manage and draw from. It is important that you refer to relevant pre-seen information in your responses as well as incorporating the unseen information.

The key things that you need to do to assimilate the information effectively and efficiently are:

- Read about and identify each event

- Consider what the issue is

- Evaluate the impact of the issue. Who is affected, by how much are they affected and what would happen if no action was taken?

- Determine the most useful and relevant exhibits from the pre-seen

Capturing all of your thoughts and ideas at this stage can be difficult and time consuming.

The following section on planning your answer will show you how to do this effectively without wasting time or effort.

4 Planning your answers

In section 2 of this chapter we saw how important it was to manage your time in the exam to ensure you're able to complete all of the necessary stages in the preparation of your answer.

One important aspect of your exam is planning your answer. Sitting the Case Study Exam is not as straight forward as turning up, reading the requirements, and then writing your answer.

If you do attempt to write without any form of content plan, your response will lack direction and a logical flow, it won't fully address the key points required and any recommendations will lack solid justification. It is for this reason that time should be specifically allocated to planning the content of your answers.

Given the preparation you've done before the exam, reading the unseen can often feel like a firework display is happening in your brain; each new piece of information you read about triggers a series of thoughts and ideas.

The planning process must therefore begin as soon as you start reading the unseen information. Every second counts within the case study exam and so it's important to use all of your time effectively by capturing the thoughts as they come to you.

To make sure the time spent now is of use to you throughout the task, you will need consider carefully how best to document your thoughts. You will be provided with an on-screen notes page ('scratchpad') as well as a wipe-clean laminated notes page and marker pen. Any method you adopt to plan must be concise whilst still allowing you to capture all of your ideas and see the bigger picture in terms of how the issues interrelate with one another (see additional guidance below). Furthermore, the method must suit you! Everyone is different and what might work for one person could be a disaster for another. For example, some people prefer to work with lists, other with mind maps.

Most people find that some form of central planning sheet (to enable the bigger picture to be seen) is best. How you prepare the central planning sheet is a matter of personal preference and we've given illustrations of two different methods below. Practise each one to find out which you prefer and then tailor it further to settle on something that works for you.

Method 1 – The ordered list

This process is ideally suited to people who prefer lists and structure.

Step 1:

- Begin by reading everything in the task exhibit
- Ensure you have identified all aspects of the task and then write this on the left hand side of your planning sheet

Step 2:

- Read everything in the trigger exhibit, making notes next to the relevant task

Step 3:

- Review your list to identify any linkages to information provided in the pre-seen and note next to the task on your planning sheet

Step 4:

- Brainstorm any technical knowledge you can use in responding to the task and note this on your planning sheet

Illustration 1 – Planning

On Monday morning your boss arrived in work full of enthusiasm for a new business venture he had thought of over the weekend. This was in response to a conversation that had taken place at Friday night drinks when the CEO expressed concern that she felt the business was stagnating and needed some new products to rekindle customer interest.

Your boss needed to harness his ideas and put together an outline plan for a mid-morning coffee meeting with the CEO. Typically, the idea had germinated without sufficient thought and you were asked to consider the critical factors that needed to be considered in launching the new product and write a briefing document for the meeting.

Requirement:

Prepare a plan for your briefing document.

Solution

Critical Factors	Goals and objectives	Skills and experience	Finance	Marketing and sales
New Product	Matches objectives?	Experience in manufacturing?	Available finance?	Advertising
	Strengths?	Available labour?	Investment?	Social media
			Working capital?	Website?
Technical content?	SFA		NPV	4Ps

Method 2 – The extended mind map

This process is ideally suited to those who prefer pictures and diagrams to trigger their thoughts.

Step 1:

- Read the unseen information and identify the key tasks required
- As you read, write each task in a "bubble" on your planning sheet.

Step 2:

- Keep adding each new part of the task you identify to your sheet. At the end you should have a page with a number of bubbles dotted about.

Step 3:

- Review your bubbles to identify any linkages to the trigger information or pre-seen exhibits. Add any relevant information to your planning sheet in a bubble attached the appropriate part of the task.

Step 4:

- Review the task bubbles and brainstorm any relevant knowledge which you can use in responding to the task. Add this to bubbles attached to the task

With detailed information provided in the exam it would be very likely that your brain would think of a wide range of ideas which, if left uncaptured, would be forgotten as quickly as you thought of them.

This is where mind mapping comes in handy. You would not of course need to draw one as neat as this and feel free to add colours or graphics to help your thought processes.

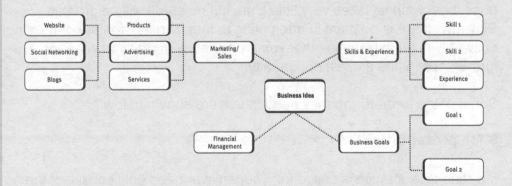

Have a go!

Why not try putting your thoughts on the previous illustration into a mind map like the one above?

Some additional guidance

(1) This is perhaps the hardest part of the exam; as soon as you tell your brain it needs to come up with some ideas, it very often refuses to cooperate! Practice makes perfect so working through the exercises in Chapter 7 and attempting mock exams will really help your brain to deliver ideas when you need it to.

(2) Don't simply view technical models as something that must be included to tick a box if explicitly requested in the requirements. Instead use the models to help analyse the issues, suggest solutions or generate ideas. They were developed to be useful!

(3) If you start looking at one of the task requirements and are stuck for ideas, don't waste time staring into space. Move on to the next part of the task (but not onto the next task itself as you won't be able to return) and you'll find the creative juices soon start flowing.

5 Communication skills

The Case Study examinations aim to test a wide range of skills and you may be required to communicate in many different formats to various different audiences, each with different information needs. How well you communicate will be awarded as both part of the integration mark but also as part of the people skills, because communication skills is a subset of people skills.

Clearly the content of what you write is far more important than the chosen format, so you needn't spend more than a few seconds on the most basic elements of presentation – there won't, for example, be a mark for inserting the date in a letter or email.

Tasks are often phrased in a conversational manner in order to reflect the manner in which instructions may be communicated in the workplace. There are no marks for responding in a similar vein. For example, wishing your boss 'best wishes' takes very little time, but no credit will be granted. Similarly, there is no point in attempting to mask an incomplete or missing answer with an explanation that you are too busy or that you will send a further reply at the earliest opportunity.

Some of the formats you may need to use are shown below.

Slide presentation

If a slide presentation is called for, your answer need only consist of the bullet points that would appear on each slide. Read the requirement carefully as guidance will be given on how many slides to prepare and the maximum number of bullets on each slide. Most likely this would be 2 slides, with a maximum of 5 bullets on each slide (or you may just be asked for 10 bullet points in total). You will not need to prepare speaker notes. You do not need to layout your answer as a slide (i.e. you don't need to draw a box). Simply noting the bullets will be sufficient.

Illustration 2 – Slides

A typical layout for the presentation of slides should be:

Slide 1

Title

- XX
- XX
- XX
- XX
- XX

Slide 2

Title

- XX
- XX
- XX
- XX
- XX

An email

A requirement to draft an email may be in response to a specific question raised by an individual within the unseen information, or perhaps even in response to an email that is presented within the unseen.

You will need to ensure you give your email a title and make it clear who it is to and who it is from.

e.g

Illustration 3 – E-mail

A typical layout for the presentation of an email should be:

> **To: XX**
> **From:XX**
> **Date: XX**
>
> **Subject: XX**
>
> Your answer to the requirement using short sentences as instructed

Headings for emails and letters etc may often be inserted at the top of the answer box, so nothing needs to be done in terms of headings.

If you are asked to write an email, then you should write short sentences (the number of which may well be specified in the requirement) and NOT brief bullet points. The headings shown in the above illustration (who the email is to, from etc) may well be given as a proforma in the exam.

A letter

Exactly the same as for an email but laid out in letter format. That means you should include a space for an address, a date, state to whom the letter is addressed and a summary of what the letter is regarding.

The letter should be signed off in the normal business fashion, unless you are told otherwise.

e.g

Illustration 4 – Letter

A typical layout for the presentation of a letter should be:

> Address
>
> Date
>
> **Dear X**
>
> **Title**
>
> Content of your answer to the requirement using short sentences or bullet points as instructed.
>
> Yours sincerely,
>
> Finance Manager

A report

In the pilot exam a commonly requested format is a report. This is likely to be an internal report but should still follow an appropriate and formal structure. The exact headings in your report will needed to be tailored to the exact task requirements but the following example is a good start:

e.g

Illustration 5 – Report

A typical layout for a report should be:

> **Title: A report on the implementation of Total Quality Management**
>
> Introduction
>
> Brief background/context for requirement
>
> Main report content broken down using further sub-headings
>
> Conclusion
>
> Key conclusions and recommendations

6 Writing style

Introduction

Writing style is something that develops over time. It is influenced by your education and experiences. To some it comes easily, they enjoy words – but remember, you are not looking to win any prizes in literature. It's about putting facts, ideas and opinions in a clear, concise, logical fashion. Some students get very worried about their writing styles. As a general rule you should try to write as you would talk.

Logical flow

A typical point starts with a statement of fact, either given in the case or derived from analysis – 'what?'

This can then be followed by an interpretation – 'so what?'

This can then lead to an implication – 'now what?', or 'what next?'

For example:

(1) What? – The NPV is positive.

(2) So what? – Suggesting we should go ahead with the project.

(3) Now what? – Arrange board meeting to discuss strategic implications.

A similar structure can be obtained using the Socratic approach – what, why, how?

- So what?
- Why should we use it?
- How does it work?

Who is reading the response?

Failure to pitch the level correctly will inevitably result in failure to communicate your ideas effectively, since the reader will either be swamped with complexity, or bored with blandness. The recipients of the report should also dictate the level of tact required

Tactless	Tactful
The directors have clearly made errors	There were other options open to the board that, with hindsight, would have been beneficial
The marketing director is responsible for this disastrous change in strategy.	The board should consider where this went wrong? It would appear that the marketing department may have made some mistakes

Making your response easy to read

To ensure that the marker finds your answers accessible and easy to read, you should try to do the following:

- Use short words, short sentences, short phrases and short paragraphs. If you are adopting the 'what, so what, what now' approach, then you could have a paragraph containing three sentences. The next point can then be a new paragraph, also containing three sentences.

- Use the correct words to explain what you mean! For example, students often get confused between:
  - recommendations (what they should do – actions) and options (what they could do – possibilities).
  - objectives (what we want to achieve – the destination) and strategies (how we intend to achieve them – the route).

- Avoid using vague generalisations. Too often students will comment that an issue will "impact" on profit rather than being specific about whether profit will increase or decrease (or even better still, trying to quantify by how much). Other common phrases which are too vague include "communicate with" (you need to say specifically what should be discussed) and "look in to" (how should an option be looked in to?).

- Avoid unnecessary repetition. This can either be of information from the exam paper (pre-seen or unseen), of discussion within the report (in particular between what is said in one section and another) or can relate to the words that you use. Some students fall into the trap of thinking that writing a professional report means simply writing more words to say the same thing! The issue is quality not quantity.

For example, compare the following:

- – 'I, myself, personally'   OR 'I'
- – 'export overseas'   OR 'export'
- – 'green in colour'   OR 'green'

- Watch your spelling – this may seem a small and unimportant point, but poor spelling makes a document seem sloppy and may convey an impression that the content is as loose as the general appearance! Poor spelling interrupts the marker as they read your report, so there is the danger that they conclude that it did not have a logical flow.

- Recommendations – be decisive – do not 'sit on the fence' or ask for more information. Make a clear recommendation based on the information you have and justify why you have chosen that course of action.

Exercise 1

This exercise will get you thinking about what makes a well written script. The technical content of the requirement is not relevant – we are focusing on writing style and flow.

> The risk committee of Xplc met to discuss a report by its risk manager. The report focused on a number of risks that applied to a chemicals factory recently acquired in another country.
>
> She explained that the new risks related to the security of the new factory in respect of burglary, the supply of one of the key raw materials that experienced fluctuations in world supply and also an environmental risk.
>
> The environmental risk was with respect to the possibility of poisonous emissions from the new factory. The CEO who chaired the risk committee, said that the factory was important to him for two reasons. First, he said it was strategically important to the company. Second, it was important because his own bonuses depended upon it. He said that he knew from the report what the risks were, but that he wanted somebody to explain to him what strategies they could use to manage the risks. 'I don't get any bonus at all until we reach a high level of output from the factory,' he said. 'So I don't care what the risks are, we will have to manage them.'

You have been asked to outline strategies that can be used to manage risk and identify, with reasons, an appropriate strategy for each of the three risks facing the new venture.

Requirement:

Consider these two responses and note the positive and negative aspects of each.

Answer 1

Risk can be managed using the TARA strategies.

- **Transfer** the risk to another organisation for example by buying insurance. This is usually cost effective where the probability of the risk is low but the impact is potentially high.
- **Avoid** the risk altogether by withdrawing completely from the risky activity. This is done where the risk is high probability and high frequency and so it is too costly to reduce the risk sufficiently.
- **Reduce** the risk by implementing controls or by diversification.
- **Accept** the risk without taking any further steps to mitigate it. For this to be acceptable the frequency and the impact of the risk must place the risk within the risk appetite of the company.

Risk of burglary

It is usual to insure against burglary an example of the transfer strategy. This is because of the high impact of burglary.

It is also usual to put safeguards in place such as security guards because of the probability of burglary. This is an example of risk reduction.

Raw Materials Supply Fluctuation

Depending on the cost benefit analysis the company could chose to transfer the risk by entering into forward contracts to purchase the materials.

There will be a cost associated with this and it will lower but not remove the risk associated with supply and price fluctuations. They may choose to accept the risk as part of the operational risk associated with their industry.

Environmental Risk

The company should take reasonable steps to reduce the chance poisonous emissions. It should use appropriate technology and controls to reduce the risk.

Risks cannot be completely eliminated so if the poisonous emissions could give rise to significant costs it should also purchase insurance and transfer the risk.

Answer Two

Risk is managed by this:

(1) Identify the risk. This is by brainstorming all the things that the risk can be.

(2) Risk assessment. We won't know this properly until afterwards

(3) Risk Profiling. This is decided on consequences and impact

(4) Risk quantification. This can be average loss or it can be largest loss.

(5) Risk consolidation which will depend on the risk appetite and diversification.

The risks at the factory are:

- The main risk at the factory is environmental risk. You can't do anything about this risk because global warming is because of everyone

- The big risk is that the CEO is "I don't care what the risks are" this will need to have the risk awareness embedded in and the tone at the top.

- The other risk is that the CEO could manipulate the output levels to get his bonus. This needs to be looked at seriously because he is also on the risk committee and the remuneration committee and he is not independent and that should be a NED.

7 Summary

You should have an appreciation of some of the issues you may encounter in the exam and some possible techniques to overcome these.

Next steps:

(1) In the next two chapters we will present the unseen and guide you through the process of producing an answer. It is worth ensuring you can log on to the Pearson Vue site now and make sure you have registered for the practice case study exam. It is advisable to familiarise yourself with the software as much as possible.

(2) As you are about to embark on a full attempt at the pilot paper it is a good time to revisit previous chapters and ensure you are comfortable with all of the material so far before proceeding.

Test your understanding answers

Exercise 1

The first solution has several positive aspects:

- Brief introduction linking to requirement
- Overview of model with explanation and clear examples
- Specific points from scenario addressed
- Headings clearly signpost the answer
- Appropriate language

There are some areas which could be improved:

- Specific reference to the company name
- More explicit use of the information from the scenario

The second solution is not as strong as the first. Some of the main criticisms:

- Main options available are not clearly explained
- No attempt to introduce the answer
- Inappropriate language for a formal report/response
- Lack of tact regarding the CEO – the intended audience!!

As a piece of writing there is not much to say from a positive perspective except:

- Clear structure
- Writing is concise (but probably a bit too brief)

9

Unseen information for the pilot case

Chapter learning objectives

The pilot case study contained the following triggers and tasks.

Note that in the exam these are not labelled as "tasks" or "triggers" but are presented simply as exhibits, emails, articles and so on. Similarly exhibits are not numbered.

Exhibit 1 – Trigger

Today's newspapers are headlining with news of a significant increase in aviation fuel prices.

Air Fares Set To Rise As Jet Fuel Prices Soar

Unrest in the Middle East pushes crude oil prices to their highest level since 2008 this week. The airline industry seems set to be the biggest casualty of this increase because rising crude oil prices mean a corresponding hike in the cost of aviation fuel.

It is not yet clear whether the airlines will increase ticket prices in response to this development or whether they will attempt to absorb the increase in the hope that fuel prices return to their earlier level.

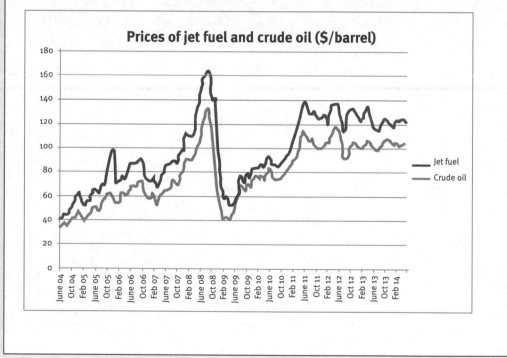

Prices of jet fuel and crude oil ($/barrel)

Exhibit 2 – Task

The Finance Director has sent you an email asking you to be part of a working party:

From: Michael Gibbons (Finance Director)
Sent: 13th Feb, 10:21 a.m.
Subject: Re: Working Party

I would like you to join a working party that has been established to consider potential ways of reducing costs and increasing revenues.

I am concerned that the scenario in which the price of aviation fuel is inflated may continue into the long term.

I would like us to suggest ways in which improved accounting might help the company to manage this problem.

Before the first meeting I would like you to prepare a report that covers two issues:

- Firstly, include a strategic analysis of the implications for Fly-jet of a prolonged increase in fuel prices.

- Secondly, include an evaluation of the ways in which the adoption of activity based management and target costing could be used to help us identify potential cost reduction opportunities.

Michael Gibbons
Finance Director
Fly-jet
E: mg@Fly-jet.co.uk
T: 0161 233 3434

Prepare a report as detailed in the Finance Director's email.

Exhibit 3 – Trigger

One week later

The working party's initial findings included the introduction of a total quality management programme (TQM). It was also suggested that the company would move towards providing some of the customer benefits that are traditionally associated with full-service airlines. In particular, Fly-jet will offer a customer loyalty scheme:

- Customers would pay a $50 fee to initially join the scheme.

- Members of the loyalty scheme would be able to redeem their joining fee by selecting their seats for free in the first 12 months of membership, saving $10 per flight, up to a maximum of 5 times.

- Members of the loyalty scheme would earn loyalty points based on the miles travelled and these points could result in free flights if a sufficient number of points are collected. It is estimated (based on similar schemes offered by others in the industry) that the free flights earned from the loyalty scheme would represent 5% of annual revenue.

Extract from the executive summary of the working party report:

Introduction of a total quality management programme

The working party considered a paper presented by the Senior Management Accountant that detailed the potential benefits to the company of the introduction of a total quality management programme. The working party recognised that other competitor airlines had already introduced this type of programme and determined that in order to remain competitive that Fly-jet should implement a similar programme as a priority.

Customer loyalty scheme

The working party considered a suggestion from the Marketing Director that the company should differentiate itself from other low-cost carriers by introducing a customer loyalty scheme. The Marketing Director informed the working party that whilst a number of the 'flag carrier' airlines offer loyalty schemes that Fly-jet would be the first of the low-cost carriers to do so. The working party agreed that this was a potential option for the company and that the Finance Director should provide further details of the financial implications of the scheme.

Exhibit 4 – Task

The Finance Director has emailed you:

From: Michael Gibbons (Finance Director)
Sent: 13th Feb, 10:21 a.m.
To: Senior Management Accountant
Subject: Re: Loyalty Scheme

I am sure that you are aware of the proposals to introduce TQM and also to extend our services to incorporate some of the features traditionally associated with full-cost airlines.

Prepare a report that demonstrates clearly the change management issues associated with introducing TQM to Fly-jet.

I am concerned that the move towards a full-service model will do very little to improve our revenues. I need you to evaluate the marketing implications of this proposal.

Michael Gibbons
Finance Director
Fly-jet
E: mg@Fly-jet.co.uk
T: 0161 233 3434

Write a report as detailed in the Finance Director's email.

Exhibit 5 – Trigger

The following announcement has been made available to all of Fly-jet's staff via the company intranet:

"Fly-jet's reports regret to announce that as of 1 January a total of 100 (equivalent full-time) posts will be made redundant. It is estimated that 70 of these posts will be of an administrative/clerical nature and that the remainder will come from junior and senior management levels.

We would like if possible to avoid forced redundancies and therefore if any staff member is interested in pursuing the option of voluntary redundancy they should contact the HR Director for more details.

We appreciate that this is a difficult time for all staff members but can assure you that we would not be considering redundancies if it was not absolutely necessary for the long term survival of the business."

Exhibit 6 – Task

The Finance Director has emailed you:

From: Michael Gibbons
Sent: 13th Feb, 10:21 a.m.
Subject: Re: Announcement

The HR director has asked the board to consider the implications of the employees' possible response to the redundancy announcement. As a related issue, the union representatives have already balloted their members over the question of a strike in protest at the redundancy announcement.

I need you to evaluate the following issues for me:

* How should the board approach the negotiation with the union representatives?

* How should we plan for the potential strike scenario?

Michael Gibbons
Finance Director
Fly-jet
E: mg@Fly-jet.co.uk
T: 0161 233 3434

Respond to the Finance Director

(Note: you were then presented with a blank email to complete)

Exhibit 7 – Trigger

One month later, the following press release was issued by Fly-jet:

Fly-jet announces the purchase of the tour operator Fly-tours

Fly-jet is pleased to announce that it has agreed a deal for the purchase of the tour operator Fly-tours. The synergies which will be achieved from the combination of the two companies will ensure that the Fly-jet group can continue to grow and maintain its competitive advantage in what is a highly competitive market. The increased load factor will enable us to keep our costs and prices low, benefiting all our customers. This deal will also provide job security for the staff of both Fly-jet and Fly-tours for the foreseeable future.

For further information, please contact the Fly-jet Press Office or log onto www.Fly-jet.com

---

Exhibit 8 – Task

The Finance Director has emailed you:

> **From:** Michael Gibbons
> **Sent:** 13th Feb, 10:21 a.m.
> **Subject:** Re: Fly-tours
>
> The purchase of Fly-tours creates some interesting problems for us. Firstly, we need to integrate Fly-tours' accounting department with our own. The greatest challenge is that their staff will have to change to our way of doing things. I need you to prepare a report on responding to this challenge.
>
> Secondly, we need to determine the fair value of Fly-tours' assets for the sake of determining goodwill on acquisition. Their main assets are aircraft and also intangible assets in the form of landing rights at various airports that Fly-tours serves. Give me a report identifying the issues associated with determining the fair values of those assets.
>
> Thirdly, there will be some transfer pricing issues arising from Fly-tours using our aircraft for their holidaymakers on some routes. We have agreed in principle that we will do that on the basis of a cost-plus arrangement. Prepare a report that discusses the most appropriate manner of determining both our costs and our mark-up for these transfer prices.
>
> **Michael Gibbons**
> Finance Director
> Fly-jet
> E: mg@Fly-jet.co.uk
> T: 0161 233 3434

Respond to the Finance Director

1 Summary

This chapter has introduced you to the unseen information for the pilot exam.

Next steps:

(1) You should work through this exam using the unseen information (ideally the online Pearson Vue version) and the following chapter, which contains lots of guidance to help you with your first attempt. The examiners consider it crucial that any practice you do, such as using the pilot paper, is treated like a real exam. You should therefore be writing out your own answers before reviewing the suggested solutions. Merely reading the requirements and then the suggested solutions has limited value.

Walkthrough of the pilot exam

Chapter learning objectives

- To understand the thought processes that will help you when working through the exam
- To have the opportunity to attempt the pilot paper with guidance

1 The Aim of a Walkthrough

The aim of this chapter is to give you a chance to practise many of the techniques you have been shown in previous chapters of this study text. This should help you to understand the various thought processes needed to complete the full three hour examination. It is important that you work through this chapter at a steady pace.

Don't rush on to the next stage until you have properly digested the information, followed the guidance labelled 'Stop and Think!' and made your own notes. This will give you more confidence than simply reading the model solutions. You should refer to the unseen produced in the previous chapter as you proceed through these exercises.

The following chapter will then guide you through the suggested solutions and marking key.

2 Summary of trigger 1

The graph presented in the unseen shows significant increases in fuel prices. There is some uncertainty whether these increases will be passed on to the customer or not.

Stop and think!

(1) Consider how this may be relevant to Flyjet

(2) What do we know about fuel costs at Flyjet?

(3) How would customers react to increases being passed on?

3 Overview of task 1

Flyjet is considering ways to increase revenue and reduce costs. It is suggested that improved accounting may help.

You are required to prepare a report covering:

* Strategic analysis of increase in fuel prices
* Evaluation of how ABM and target costing can help identify cost reduction opportunities.

Let's plan

We need to create a planning page that ensures you identify and respond to all parts of the requirement. You can use the techniques discussed in Chapter Eight or develop your own method. Here we will use the ordered list approach.

Split your planning sheet (use your wipe clean whiteboard) in two – one half for each part of the task, and then split the second section down further as follows:

Strategic analysis of fuel price increase
How ABM can help identify cost reduction opportunities
How target costing can help identify cost reduction opportunities

Note that the first section is roughly twice the size of the other two as we are assuming that each main task heading is equally weighted. But we have split down the second part of the task further to ensure we cover both ABM and target costing.

You now need to brainstorm all the relevant points you can think of under the above headings, making sure you are bringing together your knowledge from the relevant syllabus as well as your analysis of the pre-seen information.

Let's think a bit more about these requirements by breaking them down into the component parts. Take the phrase 'strategic analysis of the implications for Flyjet of a prolonged increase in fuel prices'.

The term 'strategic analysis' means that we need to consider how the increased fuel prices affect WHAT we do (strategically) rather than HOW we do things (operationally). 'For Flyjet' highlights that our answer needs to be specific to this company rather than a general answer.

Why have they mentioned 'prolonged increase'? Well we need to think about whether Flyjet can absorb these additional costs in the long term and if not, how customers may react to increased prices.

As a rough rule of thumb you should spend about 15–20% of the time available for reading and planning. So for this section of the exam, where you are given 45 minutes, you should be spending approximately 7–8 minutes planning your answer before you complete the exercise below. This would leave you about 35 minutes to write your answer and a few minutes spare to check through what you have written.

Exercise – 1
Prepare a response to the first task in the pilot exam Flyjet.

4 Summary of trigger 2

Following on from the previous trigger and task there are several suggestions made within Flyjet to reduce costs and increase revenues. This trigger introduces the ideas of TQM (to maintain competitive advantage) and a customer loyalty scheme to differentiate from other low-cost carriers - as no others have done this yet.

Stop and think!

(1) No need to consider benefits of TQM as this has already been done - need to think implementation

(2) Think about your experiences with low cost airlines. Would a customer loyalty scheme encourage you?

(3) It is suggested that the company starts to move towards a full service model – have any other real life airlines done this? Successfully?

5 Summary of task 2

You are required to prepare a report covering:

*   Report on change management issues associated with introducing TQM to Flyjet.

*   Evaluate the marketing implications of move towards a 'full service' model

Let's plan

In the previous exercise we used an ordered list to plan the answer. We could easily use a mind map here to collect our thoughts and ensure all areas are covered. Draw a circle on your whiteboard about a third of the way down the page and write in it 'change management re TQM'. Then two thirds of the way down the page draw another circle and write in it 'marketing implications of full service model'.

Be careful not to paraphrase too much as you could end up not properly planning your answer or addressing the requirement when you write your response. For example if you just wrote 'marketing implications' it is very likely you would go off on a tangent focusing too much on the customer loyalty scheme and not fully answering the question.

Your planning page would start off looking like this:

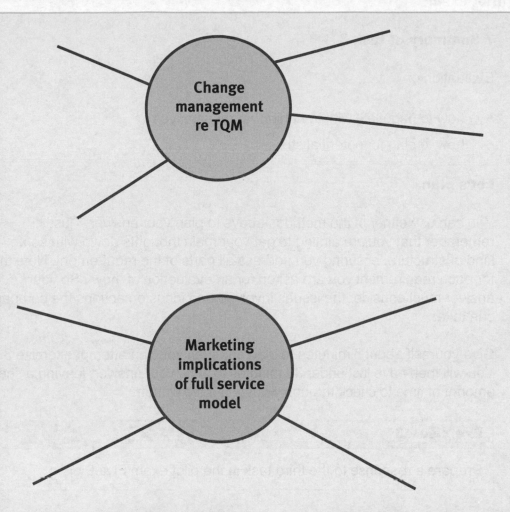

Now spend 6-7 minutes completing your plan before attempting Exercise 2.

You would then have 30 minutes to write your answer and a few minutes to check through what you have written before reviewing the solution.

Exercise – 2

Prepare a response to the second task in the pilot exam Flyjet.

6 Summary of trigger 3

An internal announcement has been made on the company Intranet explaining that 100 redundancies will take place in admin and management posts. The announcement requests applications for voluntary redundancy and also states that these redundancies are necessary for the long term survival of the business.

Stop and think!

(1) Remember this workforce is unionised – what are the implications?

(2) Think about the impact of this if it happened in your company

7 Summary of task 3

Evaluation of:

- how to negotiate with the union representatives
- how to plan for potential strike

Let's plan

You can use either of the methods above to plan your answer – just remember that you are aiming to get your main thoughts down with some kind of structure, ensuring you address all parts of the requirement. Note that for each requirement you are asked for an evaluation of 'how'. So your answer must consider the issues involved and focus on actions the company can take.

Give yourself about 5 minutes to plan and then you can attempt exercise 3. You will then have just under 30 minutes to write your answer, leaving a short amount of time to check through what you have written.

Exercise – 3
Prepare a response to the third task in the pilot exam Flyjet.

8 Summary of trigger 4

You are given a press release announcing the acquisition of a tour operator Fly-tours. The release explains the synergies that are expected including increased load factor and improved job security.

Stop and think!

(1) The deal has already been agreed – so won't require a long list of benefits or evaluation of whether it should go ahead. Expect an implementation based task

(2) Do you understand increased load factor? The tour customers will represent guaranteed seat bookings on certain flights.

(3) You should thinking of this issue in light of the recent redundancies

9 Summary of task 4

You are asked to prepare:

*   a report on the challenge of integrating two accounting departments

*   a report identifying issues with determining the fair values of aircraft and landing rights

*   a report discussing manner of determining costs and mark-ups for flight transfer prices

Let's plan

This is quite a complex section and you have sixty minutes to complete it so it's important that you manage your time carefully here. Start by splitting your time into three twenty minute blocks. For a series of reports such as these, which don't have much crossover in terms of content it is probably better to plan and write your answer to the first part before you move on to planning the next section – this should prevent you from getting too confused and will ensure you cover each part.

You will inevitably score higher with this section if you attempt each report in some way rather than providing a comprehensive answer to one part and running out of time to complete the final part.

For the first report it is worth thinking about what would happen if this was your company. What would the challenges be and how could they be overcome. Note the question is about integrating the departments not just the systems so you also need to consider staff issues.

Don't get scared that the second report is asking for something highly technical just because it uses the phrase 'fair value'! The fair value of an asset can be thought of as what it's worth to the company. So put yourself in the position of a Flyjet accountant. How could you value an aircraft or landing rights – why might this task be difficult?

For the final report be careful that you don't stray into a general discussion of all the various transfer pricing methods. A cost plus method has been agreed in principle and this needs to be examined further to determine how the 'cost' and the 'plus' can be determined.

Exercise – 4

Prepare a response to the fourth task in the pilot exam Flyjet.

10 Summary

You should now have a better understanding of how to approach the exam requirements and plan your answer. Although this chapter uses the pilot exam as an example, the techniques used can be applied to any set of exam tasks.

Next steps:

(1) As previously mentioned you should attempt a written answer yourself to all of the tasks before reviewing the suggested solutions.

(2) Reviewing the solutions may highlight knowledge gaps which you may need to revisit.

Test your understanding answers

Exercise – 1

> These answers have been provided by CIMA for information purposes only. The answers created are indicative of a response that could be given by a good candidate. They are not to be considered exhaustive, and other appropriate relevant responses would receive credit.
>
> CIMA will not accept challenges to these answers on the basis of academic judgement.

Section 1

Report to the finance director

Strategic implications of an increase in fuel prices and an evaluation of activity-based management

Fuel prices

The price of aviation fuel continues to be volatile. The political situation in major oil exporting countries has caused a recent spike in prices. This paper discusses some of the implications of a prolonged increase.

Fuel accounts for 1.7/6.8 = 25% of our cost per ASK (see pre-seen). That suggests that a prolonged increase will prove costly to our operations.

Given the central role of fuel prices in the industry, we can expect to see other airlines increasing ticket prices in response to this increase in cost. It may be that we can consider passing on the increased cost of airfares to customers because prices will be rising across the industry.

Unfortunately, our position as a no-frills airline does not save us a significant amount in terms of fuel costs and so we may lose ground to the traditional airlines. For example, National Air's fuel cost is only 1.8/9.6 = 19% of their cost per ASK. In other words, if we both pass on the same cost increase for fuel our fares will rise by a larger proportion than theirs and so we could lose some of our competitive position.

Clearly, many of our customers are forced to buy airline tickets and so a price rise will leave a segment of the market unaffected. Unfortunately, there are also customers who have some discretion over whether to travel (or travel is a luxury). We can expect total demand to decline in the event of a price rise. Again, that could erode some of our competitive advantage because running our aircraft at close to full capacity helps us to offer lower prices than our competitors.

ABM and target costing

Our use of ZBB (see pre-seen) and other techniques mean that we would have to do very little in order to move further towards the use of activity based management and target costing. Arguably, we have used both techniques to a large extent albeit under a different heading.

Activity based management requires that we understand the cost of providing our service. The biggest area in which we might explore that is by looking at our route network and the costs of operating from specific airports. Clearly, some routes will always be more profitable than others. Some airports charge higher landing fees and so the profitability of routes cannot be directly compared.

ABM would require us to study costs and revenues closely with a view to making a decision as to whether we could utilise resources more effectively. For example, we should study customers' buying behaviour to establish whether we have routes that feed into other services. For example, some routes may appear to be relatively unprofitable but they stimulate demand because passengers then fly on to a final destination using Fly-jet. Closing some routes may lead to a more significant loss of revenue when the onward connections are taken into account.

ABM might also help us to understand the impact of some of the processes that we use. For example, the sale of inflight snacks is difficult to cost because we are using flight attendants who would be paid anyway, but they could lead to unseen costs, such as additional cleaning costs and potential delays when readying a plane for its next flight.

Target costing would be useful because there are market forces that restrict our prices. We are likely to find it difficult to sell tickets if our competitors undercut us. We must also offer some consistency in our pricing because our prices are visible on the website and customers may be concerned that prices are excessive if routes are priced differently for flights of a similar duration.

To an extent, target costing is difficult because we cannot manage all costs. For example, engineering costs are difficult to reduce without compromising flight safety.

We are also a victim of our own success because we have already cut many costs to the absolute minimum and have eliminated many of the discretionary costs that have been identified as avoidable. It may be possible to introduce cost reductions by stealth, such as gradually increasing the selling prices of our inflight snack range or by selling more services such as premier seats.

I hope that this report is helpful. Please contact me if you have any questions.

Exercise – 2

Report to the finance director

Change management and marketing issues

Move to TQM

TQM may prove threatening to our staff because our business model is essentially to keep costs to the bare minimum. Improving on cost may lead to redundancy because staff costs are our second greatest component of cost per ASK and engineering is also labour intensive.

TQM traditionally involves staff being involved in quality circles and similar activities. Our business makes that difficult because aircrew travel and are rarely able to meet with colleagues other than those in their aircraft. It may be possible to circumvent that by communicating through email or via teleconference.

It may be difficult for us to fully understand our customers' needs in this context. We accept that many of our customers' feel that we offer a less exciting and desirable service than is available from the full-cost airlines. Moving towards meeting those concerns would be difficult to accomplish without incurring additional cost, which would be unacceptable. We would have to take great care to ensure that we do not raise unrealistic expectations through this exercise.

Staff may be concerned that we will aim to raise customer satisfaction levels with a product that is quite deliberately cut back to the minimum. We aim to provide value for money, but we do not aim to meet our competitors' levels of service because it would be too expensive to do so (see pre-seen).

Marketing implications

Successful marketing implies identifying and satisfying customer needs.

The need that we aim to meet is for inexpensive and efficient air travel. We offer a product that is differentiated largely on price. To an extent, we signal that fact by making our service as basic as possible, consistent with safety and meeting basic minimum standards of comfort.

Adding services such as those that have been proposed might create the impression that Fly-jet's service should be compared with that offered by the traditional, full service airlines. On that basis, we will suffer in the comparison because we cannot match their service on quality or convenience.

Having said that the traditional airlines are attempting to cut costs in order to be more competitive with the budget airlines and so the distinction is eroding anyway (see pre-seen).

The proposal may be misinterpreted as an attempt to generate net revenues. Customers have to pay an additional sum for those services and may feel that the cost is excessive. That may lead to a cynical sense that we are simply trying to exploit our customers. The danger is that we would have very little uptake and so have the cost of running the scheme for the sake of a small number of participants.

If the changes can be promoted adequately then we will possibly have a significant advantage because customers may fly with us in preference to our competitors for the sake of accruing loyalty points. The fact that they have paid for this membership will make earning the points all the more important to them.

I hope that this report is helpful. Please contact me if you have any questions.

Exercise – 3

Negotiation

Unfortunately, these proposals follow on from a period in which the company has already been forced to make staff redundant (see pre-seen). Our starting point will be to gain the union representatives' trust in our commitment to the job security of the remaining staff.

We can expect the unions to be wary because we have already sought volunteers for redundancy and were forced to make staff redundant against their will in the last round of rightsizing. Even if we agree to minimise the number of compulsory redundancies, that is unlikely to mean much because there are unlikely to be any volunteers.

It may be necessary to offer to provide an attractive redundancy package. If we offer generous terms then the unions may be more willing to cooperate because some staff may be willing to volunteer for an enhanced offer. If the financial cost of such a scheme would be too great then we could possibly offer non-cash incentives such as the provision of training programmes to make staff employable in other industries.

We should also be prepared to justify the need for cuts to the unions. If they can see that the alternative is a threat of corporate failure, under which all staff would lose their jobs then it may be preferable to recommend redundancies in order to protect the remaining jobs. Part of that line of negotiation would be the discussion of a medium-term business plan that would indicate the full extent of the cuts, with evidence that the company expected to be able to maintain staffing levels.

It might be possible to persuade the unions by extending redundancies to some senior managers as a sign that the company really does not see any alternative to job cuts.

Planning for strike action

The first thing that we need to establish is whether the unions have the ability to call staff out on strike. Have there been strikes in the past? Or have there been any failed attempts to call a strike? Supervisors should be asked to talk to their staff and to report back to the HR department on their impressions of the mood of the staff.

How many staff are members of the union? It is unlikely that non-members will strike.

What areas of the business will be affected? If the strikers are administrative staff then we can cover their absence by drawing staff from other areas. If flight staff strike then they cannot be replaced by untrained and unqualified staff because of safety regulations.

Contingency plans should be developed, including ranking the urgency of different areas. For example, some departments could bring the company to a halt if the affected, say, flight operations. Those departments would have to be maintained, if possible, by using senior managers or reassigning staff from less urgent duties.

The company should contact recruitment agencies to establish the availability of suitable temporary staff. It may be unduly provocative to bring in outsiders from the outset of the strike, but it would be comforting to have the means to do so if the action was prolonged.

Exercise – 4

Section 4

Integration

The biggest obstacle to a successful integration is that the new subsidiary may have a different culture to Fly-jet. The first priority is to make it clear, hopefully in a constructive way, that integration is necessary and that it will occur. If Fly-tours staff realise that they have no alternative then they will not resist the change.

Fly-jet's accounting staff should study Fly-tour's business and its accounting systems and processes. The two businesses are quite different, even though they are both about travel. It is important that any changes made in Fly-tours are going to serve a valid business function and are not going to compromise efficient operations.

There will also be technical issues that will have to be decided, such as software packages and reconciliation of data. Ideally, it will be possible to export Fly-tour's data into Fly-jet's system and move the staff so that the previous system continues, albeit on a larger scale.

Fair values

There are relatively few models of civil aircraft and there is a worldwide market for second hand planes. It will be relatively easy to establish a fair value for Fly-tour's aircraft by contacting brokers.

The forthcoming introduction of a new model of plane (see pre-seen) could complicate matters. If the new plane is significantly better then Fly-tour's fleet could lose value because airlines prefer to buy the new model and also because they sell their existing planes early in order to upgrade. That would create a glut of the old model on the second hand market and prices would decline.

The landing slots will be far more difficult to value because they are unlikely to be traded frequently. That means that there will not be an observable market against which to measure values.

If airlines tend to change routes and abandon airlines then an airport could become less popular and so demand for landing slots could vanish unexpectedly.

The historical cost of landing rights is unlikely to have any ongoing meaning because these rights last for several years and demand could change dramatically within that period.

Transfer pricing

The first issue is the motivational issues within the company. If the cost-plus price is viewed as excessive then Fly-tours' management will be demotivated and Fly-jet's will be demotivated if it is too high.

The costs of operating an aircraft include depreciation and other costs that are determined by accounting estimates. That means that any cost-plus arrangement may arouse the suspicions of at least one party.

The fact that there is a healthy charter market may create problems if Fly-tours believes that Fly-jet is charging more than the price offered by third parties. That could lead to dysfunctional behaviour if Fly-tours manage to lease aircraft externally.

The other issue is external perspectives, particularly tax. Tax authorities will often suspect that transfer prices between fellow group members are intended to move profit from one company to another in a tax-efficient manner. The tax authorities will only accept cost-plus if it is a reasonable approximation to the price that would be charged in an arm's length transaction.

Review of solution to pilot case and marking guide

Chapter learning objectives

- To gain a deeper understanding of the way case study is marked so that you can write your answer in the exam to score more highly.

1 Introduction

As we have already explained in previous chapters the case study examinations are marked against a series of competencies. It is important that you understand this process to ensure you maximise your marks in the exam.

Once you have reviewed Chapter ten, attempted the exercises and reviewed the suggested solutions this chapter takes you through the detail of how these exercises would be marked. We have also a sample student script to show some possible strengths and weaknesses which you may recognise in your own answer.

Note: The CIMA official marking guide for the pilot case is given as follows:

Competency	Section/task	Marks	Total marks available for competency
Technical skills	(1) Activity based management	12	37
	(3) Integrating accounts department	8	
	(3) Fair value accounting	7	
	(3) Transfer pricing	7	
	Integration	3	
Business skills	(1) Strategic analysis	11	24
	(2) Marketing implications	11	
	Integration	2	
People skills	(3) Negotiation with unions	12	25
	(3) Planning for strike	11	
	Integration	2	
Leadership skills	(2) Change management	12	14
	Integration	2	

In this chapter we try to show how these marks could have been awarded/won.

2 Exam section 1

As we saw in the previous chapter the first section you were required to prepare a report covering:

- Strategic analysis of increase in fuel prices

- Evaluation of how ABM and target costing can help identify cost reduction opportunities.

Let's examine each of these areas in turn.

Strategic analysis of increase in fuel prices

It is important to recognise that such a strategic analysis is largely testing your Business Skill. You therefore need to consider your understanding of this organisation, the external environment in which it operates and any industry analysis which you may have performed when working through the pre-seen information.

This part of the requirement is asking you to consider the implications of such an increase and how it might affect what Flyjet does. This whole section is allocated 45 minutes so for this part of the exercise you have approximately 22 minutes. Working on a rough ratio of 2 marks for every point you make, this implies you need to make about 11 points. However this is not necessarily 11 separate discrete ideas. At this level a large part of the value of your answer is in explaining the implications of what you are saying.

- The first few sentences of the suggested solution introduce the context and topic of the report. We then have a section explaining the level of fuel costs at Flyjet:

  "Fuel accounts for 1.7/6.8 = 25% of our cost per ASK (see pre-seen). That suggests that a prolonged increase will prove costly to our operations."

  This earns our first two marks – one for giving the proportion of fuel costs in Flyjet and then one for explaining the implication of this.

- The next paragraph begins with the sentence:

  "Given the central role of fuel prices in the industry, we can expect to see other airlines increasing ticket prices in response to this increase in cost."

So this is the first implication of the increase in fuel prices – that other airlines may pass the cost onto customers. At this point you could move on to another new point but it will be more useful to stop and think here of the implications of the point you have made. This will help you to delve deeper into the issue and add more value to your answer. It is often helpful to ask yourself the question 'so what?'

We have made the point that other airlines may well increase their ticket prices – so what? What does this mean for Flyjet? Well we can go on to say:

"It may be that we can consider passing on the increased cost of airfares to customers because prices will be rising across the industry"

This explains the implication of our previous point and will earn an additional mark. This adds depth to our answer. Breadth of points is also important and so we can now move on to the next point which is:

"our position as a no-frills airline does not save us a significant amount in terms of fuel costs and so we may lose ground to the traditional airlines"

- We have information in the pre-seen about a more traditional airline, National Air, so it is worth including some analysis of this information here to add further weight to the point we have made. So the following comment earns a further mark:

"For example, National Air's fuel cost is only 1.8/9.6 = 19% of their cost per ASK"

This point now needs concluding so we can finish off by stating:

" In other words, if we both pass on the same cost increase for fuel our fares will rise by a larger proportion than theirs and so we could lose some of our competitive position."

- At this point it is worth returning to the requirement to think about what to discuss next. We are looking at the strategic implications of the fuel price increase. We have considered how our competitors might react. We should now turn our attention to the customers. The final paragraph can be broken down into a series of linked comments, each earning a mark. The section begins:

"many of our customers are forced to buy airline tickets and so a price rise will leave a segment of the market unaffected"

So this considers customers, such as business users and those with family overseas, who have to travel. More importantly though the company has to consider customers who can choose, as this is where the risk to Flyjet's revenue stream arises. The following point will therefore earn a further mark:

"Unfortunately, there are also customers who have some discretion over whether to travel (or travel is a luxury)."

Remember to ask yourself 'so what?' to further develop your argument. So here we can consider what this means for Flyjet and make the following point:

"We can expect total demand to decline in the event of a price rise."

- Finally we can conclude this section by saying:

"Again, that could erode some of our competitive advantage because running our aircraft at close to full capacity helps us to offer lower prices than our competitors."

We have now seen how the eleven marks for the Business Skill have been marked within this task. There are also integration marks available for this generic competency but we will consider integration later on in this chapter.

Evaluation of how ABM and target costing can help identify cost reduction opportunities

This requirement is more focused on Technical Skills core accounting and finance skills so it is going to be important to bring in your relevant technical knowledge but even more important that you apply it appropriately to the situation.

As we are assuming that there are a similar amount of marks available for this part of the section we are aiming for approximately eleven points again.

We will separate our answer into ABM and target costing to ensure all areas are properly addressed.

- The first point introduces the topic but makes a relevant link back to information from the pre-seen and will therefore earn a mark.

"Our use of ZBB (see pre-seen) and other techniques mean that we would have to do very little in order to move further towards the use of activity based management and target costing"

- We can then go on to consider ABM in more detail, beginning with an implication for Flyjet:

"Activity based management requires that we understand the cost of providing our service."

To earn a mark here we need to think about costs at Flyjet – it is important to avoid merely 'textbook' answers. So to cement the point we can go on to say:

"The biggest area in which we might explore that is by looking at our route network and the costs of operating from specific airports."

thus earning a full mark.

We can then go on to consider this point in more detail and address the practicalities to earn a further mark:

"Clearly, some routes will always be more profitable than others. Some airports charge higher landing fees and so the profitability of routes cannot be directly compared."

- We can continue with an exploration of the impact on revenues:

"ABM would require us to study costs and revenues closely with a view to making a decision as to whether we could utilise resources more effectively. For example, we should study customers' buying behaviour to establish whether we have routes that feed into other services."

Again the example which links back to Flyjet is important to earning the mark here, avoiding another textbook answer.

We can continue with an example of what this customer behaviour might entail to clarify our point and earn a further mark:

"For example, some routes may appear to be relatively unprofitable but they stimulate demand because passengers then fly on to a final destination using Fly-jet. Closing some routes may lead to a more significant loss of revenue when the onward connections are taken into account."

- Finally take a step back, return to the requirement and consider any other costs which ABM may help to reduce. We have earned a mark by suggesting the following:

"ABM might also help us to understand the impact of some of the processes that we use. For example, the sale of inflight snacks is difficult to cost because we are using flight attendants who would be paid anyway, but they could lead to unseen costs, such as additional cleaning costs and potential delays when readying a plane for its next flight."

but any sensible suggestion here would earn a mark. It is important to remember that the marking guides are not rigid and credit can be earned for a variety of different responses.

- Moving on to target costing we can begin with the key benefit of using such an approach:

"Target costing would be useful because there are market forces that restrict our prices. We are likely to find it difficult to sell tickets if our competitors undercut us."

Then we can consider the implication of this and bring in the impact of our customer reactions for a further mark:

"We must also offer some consistency in our pricing because our prices are visible on the website and customers may be concerned that prices are excessive if routes are priced differently for flights of a similar duration."

To ensure we present a balanced discussion we can bring in a potential problem with target costing as applied to Flyjet:

"To an extent, target costing is difficult because we cannot manage all costs. For example, engineering costs are difficult to reduce without compromising flight safety."

- Finally we can present a few concluding points which together are worth 2 marks:

"We are also a victim of our own success because we have already cut many costs to the absolute minimum and have eliminated many of the discretionary costs that have been identified as avoidable. It may be possible to introduce cost reductions by stealth, such as gradually increasing the selling prices of our inflight snack range or by selling more services such as premier seats."

We have now seen how the eleven marks for technical skills are allocated within this section of the task. As before there are integration marks within this generic competency which we will consider later.

Following this detailed analysis of the marking guide for the first section we will now show you a suggested breakdown of the marks for the remaining tasks in the pilot exam.

3 Exam section 2

From the previous chapter we saw that this section required the following:

- Report on change management issues associated with introducing TQM to Flyjet.

- Evaluate the marketing implications of move towards a 'full service' model

Requirement		Marks
Change management issues		
	Staff feel threatened	1
	Redundancy risk	1
	Why staff costs are so important	1
	Why business doesn't support quality techniques	1
	How to overcome problems	1
	Customers' needs	1
	Customer perception	1
	Balance of full service and cost	1
	Risk of unrealistic expectations	1
	Staff concerns	1
	Our aims	1
	Link to competitors aims	1
Total – leadership skills		*12*

Requirement		Marks
Marketing implications		
	Define successful marketing	1
	Flyjet customer needs	1
	How Flyjet meets needs	1
	Impact of additional services	1
	Link to full service airlines	1
	Narrowing of gap	1
	Customer response	1
	Implications of response	1
	Importance of promotion	1
	Relevance of loyalty scheme	2
Total – business skills		*11*

Exercise – 1

The following answer represents a possible student response to Section 2:

Change management – TQM

Total Quality Management is something which ensures quality throughout the organisation. It involves using techniques such as quality circles to get it right first time and avoid defects where possible. Within TQM there are four main types of cost – prevention, appraisal, internal failure and external failure. TQM aims to minimise failure costs.

TQM might be difficult to implement in companies as it is a major change and individuals resist change. There are techniques which can be used to manage the change and overcome the resistance.

Flyjet staff have experience redundancies recently and are therefore likely to be feeling unsettled and insecure. A further (and major) change such as implementing TQM may make this worse and cause greater demotivation.

However it is possible that the employees will welcome this change as a way of improving business performance and may therefore embrace the change.

To break down the resistance to change the management should explain to the employees why the change is necessary and the benefits for the company.

Change management – TQM

Marketing implications

Flyjet are currently a no-frills airline which means they do not offer the sort of additional services which a traditional airline might do. They charge lower prices and aim to sell as many seats as possible to generate a profit. Any additional services offered incur extra charges. Flyjet are considering offering some of these additional services, for example a customer loyalty scheme.

A customer loyalty scheme would help to understand customer buying patterns and this would help Flyjet to tailor their product to the customers' interests. They could use this information in marketing campaigns to try and sell more flights.

Marketing means that Flyjet need to understand what their customers want and make sure they deliver this. The company needs to make sure their marketing message highlights what they are offering to customers. They also need to determine if their customers actually want additional services (at an additional cost potentially) or if they are simply looking for the cheapest possible flights

Requirement:

Determine the likely marks awarded for this answer.

Remember that the marking guide is not rigid and any sensible and relevant point can score credit.

4 Exam section 3

This task required an evaluation of:

- how to negotiate with the union representatives
- how to plan for potential strike

Requirement		Marks
Negotiation with unions		
	Historical context	1
	Objective of negotiation	1
	Likely resistance	1
	Problems with voluntary redundancy	1
	Incentives	1
	Implication of incentives	1
	Cost issues	1
	Alternatives	1
	Justification of cuts	1
	Possible corporate failure	1
	Business plans	1
	Management commitment to future	1
Total – people skills		*12*

Requirement		Marks
Planning for strike		
	History of strikes	1
	Perception of staff mood	1
	Potential volume of union members	1
	Job roles	1
	Opportunities for cover	1
	Safety issues	1
	Identify risk areas	1
	Contingency planning	1
	Temporary cover	1
	Implications	2
Total – business skills		*11*

5 Exam section 4

This section requires:

- a report on the challenge of integrating two accounting departments
- a report identifying issues with determining the fair values of aircraft and landing rights
- a report discussing manner of determining costs and mark-ups for flight transfer prices

Requirement		Marks
Integrating accounts department		
	Different culture	1
	Resistance by staff	1
	Reasons for change	1
	Understanding of business	1
	Differences between companies	1
	Technical issues	1
	Transfer of data	1
	Location of accounting staff	1
Total – technical skills		8

Requirement		Marks
Issues with determining fair values		
	Limited range of aircraft values	1
	Change in model	1
	Impact on values	1
	Excess supply of old planes	1
	Infrequent sales of landing slots	1
	Changes in demand	1
	Historical cost	1
Total – technical skills		7

Requirement		Marks
Transfer pricing		
	Motivation issues	1
	Fairness	1
	Accounting estimates	1
	External market pricing	1
	Dysfunctional behaviour	1
	Tax issues	1
	Arms-length transaction	1
Total – technical skills		7

6 Integration

There are 9 integration marks available in the pilot paper with marks spread across each of the generic competencies.

These marks will be awarded for the overall quality of your answer and use of available information. You should consider the style and language you use and ensure it is suitable for the intended recipient. It is also important that your responses are appropriately structured and logical.

You need to ensure that you integrate relevant parts of each of the three technical syllabi to score well here – don't view a task as just covering one of the underlying papers. Instead look for opportunities to cover more than one paper at a time – for example, how could a decision (P2) affect staff morale (E2)?

7 Summary

You should now have an understanding of how the case studies are marked which is crucial if you are going to improve your performance. It is very important that you understand what will (and won't) earn credit in the exam.

You need to master the art of writing a clear and relevant response to triggers beforehand so that you can just get on with it once the real exam starts, without wasting time.

Next steps:

(1) Revisit any chapters which you found tricky.

(2) Await the 'live' pre-seen for your exam.

(3) Re-perform the suggestions in this textbook using the real pre-seen to ensure you are prepared for the exam.

(4) Consider choosing a study option which gives you access to practice mocks – an important stage in your exam preparation.

Test your understanding answers

Exercise – 1

Answer	Marker's comments	Marks
Change management issues		
Total Quality Management is something which ensures quality throughout the organisation. It involves using techniques such as quality circles to get it right first time and avoid defects where possible.	This comment is knowledge based and misses the point of the requirement – change management	0
Within TQM there are four main types of cost – prevention, appraisal, internal failure and external failure. TQM aims to minimise failure costs.	More detail on TQM knowledge will not score any marks unless it is linked to the requirement and the scenario	0
TQM might be difficult to implement in companies as it is a major change and individuals resist change.	This shows a difficulty regarding the implementation of TQM	1
There are techniques which can be used to manage the change and overcome the resistance.	There is an attempt to answer 'so what?' regarding how can the company deal with the above difficulty – however it is vague and not specific to Flyjet	0
Flyjet staff have experience redundancies recently and are therefore likely to be feeling unsettled and insecure.	This brings in knowledge from the pre-seen and explains why there may be so much resistance	1

A further (and major) change such as implementing TQM may make this worse and cause greater demotivation.	This explains the 'so what' of the above point	1
However it is possible that the employees will welcome this change as a way of improving business performance and may therefore embrace the change.	This explains the 'so what' of the above point	1
To break down the resistance to change the management should explain to the employees why the change is necessary and the benefits for the company.	This is an attempt to discuss how to overcome resistance at Flyjet – more marks could have been earned if this was explored in more detail	1
Total marks awarded		**5**
Total available – leadership skills		*12*

Answer	Marker's comments	Marks
Marketing implications		
Flyjet are currently a no-frills airline which means they do not offer the sort of additional services which a traditional airline might do. They charge lower prices and aim to sell as many seats as possible to generate a profit.	This is simply describing the company	0
Any additional services offered incur extra charges. Flyjet are considering offering some of these additional services, for example a customer loyalty scheme.	This is describing information from the unseen	0

A customer loyalty scheme would help to understand customer buying patterns and this would help Flyjet to tailor their product to the customers' interests.	This is a marketing implication of a customer loyalty scheme – although a better answer would start with addressing the wider issue of offering additional services	1
They could use this information in marketing campaigns to try and sell more flights.	This covers the 'so what' of the previous point	1
Marketing means that Flyjet need to understand what their customers want and make sure they deliver this. The company needs to make sure their marketing message highlights what they are offering to customers.	This would have been better as an introductory point and suggests a lack of planning as there is little logic to this answer	0
They also need to determine if their customers actually want additional services (at an additional cost potentially) or if they are simply looking for the cheapest possible flights	This is an important point which could have been explored further to earn more marks.	1
Total marks awarded	**Fail**	**4**
Total available – business skills		*11*

March 2015 Exam – preseen information

Background

Bild is the third largest construction company in its home country of Ceeland. Constructmore is its biggest competitor.

Bild's activities can be categorised as civil engineering, development and investment, each of which is undertaken by a separate subsidiary.

Civil engineering

Bild's principal business activity is undertaking civil engineering projects for clients, building offices, roads and other infrastructure developments. This is a highly competitive market, but Bild is well established and has a good reputation.

Clients generally invite construction companies to bid for construction contracts on a competitive basis. Some contracts require Bild to construct a project according to a client's specification while others require Bild to assist the client with the design work prior to construction. Bild has its own professional surveyors and civil engineers and also has good contacts with outside professionals such as firms of architects, who can be brought in whenever required.

Development

Bild has some speculative ventures of its own. It buys land as an investment. Sometimes it builds projects such as office blocks with a view to finding a buyer once the building is completed.

Investment

Bild has a separate subsidiary that owns buildings that Bild retains for investment purposes. These buildings are usually rented out to third parties. Whenever Bild's development subsidiary cannot find a buyer for one of its completed buildings it will transfer that building to the investment subsidiary. The investment subsidiary generates rental income from these buildings, with a view to selling them at a profit whenever market conditions are favourable.

A typical civil engineering project

Firstly, the client specifies the project. Sometimes the client commissions the design work from its own architects and civil engineers or from independent firms offering those services. Sometimes the design work will be part of the construction project that is awarded to the construction company. A major project can take several years from initial design to final completion.

The client will normally invite several civil engineering companies to bid for the construction contract. Bid documentation will include building specification, timescales for construction work and cost forecasts. Bild has to decide whether or not it wishes to bid for a contract. It takes a great deal of time to prepare a bid and if Bild is already heavily committed to other projects, or if the project appears unlikely to generate a profit, then Bild may decline to bid. A typical project undertaken by Bild Civil Engineering will take between two and five years to complete.

If Bild is awarded a contract then a project management team is appointed. Bild's project manager will be in overall command of the project. Depending on the nature and complexity of the project, the project manager may be assisted by engineers and architects as and when required. The actual construction work is usually undertaken by subcontractors. Subcontractors generally specialise in specific areas such as laying roads or brickwork. Bild is responsible for employing any subcontractors and for paying them. Bild is also responsible for the quality of the subcontractors' work and for the prompt completion of any tasks assigned to them.

Bild must also purchase whatever materials are required and meet any other costs associated with the project.

Construction equipment is generally hired for a particular project or the subcontractors may use their own equipment. Generally, the client pays for the land and all other costs are the responsibility of the construction company.

The client will normally have the right to have the work inspected periodically by its own experts. The contract with the client is normally divided into a sequence of stages and the client will pay for the work as each agreed stage is completed. These "progress payments" will require the client's agreement that the work has been completed and is of an acceptable quality.

Once the project is completed it is handed over to the client and Bild issues a final invoice for the balance of the contract price. Typically, the contract will allow the client to withhold a small percentage of the total price (usually 3% – 5%) for an agreed period, (e.g. a year) after completion. This "retention money" will be paid at the end of the agreed period provided Bild deals with any problems that arise after the work is completed. It is common for small defects to appear because the new building settles and so it is necessary for the construction company to carry out remedial work.

Ceeland

Bild is based in the country of Ceeland. Ceeland's currency is the dollar ($).

Ceeland has adopted International Financial Reporting Standards.

Ceeland is a prosperous country. It is an island but has good international trading links.

Ceeland's capital city (Capital City) is located in the South East of the country. Most of the country's heavy industry and manufacturing is located in the North. The South West region is rural and mostly agricultural.

Ceeland's climate is temperate with a rainy season from November to February.

Job description

You are the senior management accountant of Bild. Your role in the organisation is to provide information to the Finance Director to enable the company's performance to be measured and for decision making purposes.

Organisation and structure

Bild has three subsidiary companies: Bild Civil Engineering, Bild Development and Bild Investment. Bild Civil Engineering has four regional subsidiaries, each responsible for its own geographical area.

Each subsidiary has its own board of directors. The CEO of each subsidiary is also a director of Bild

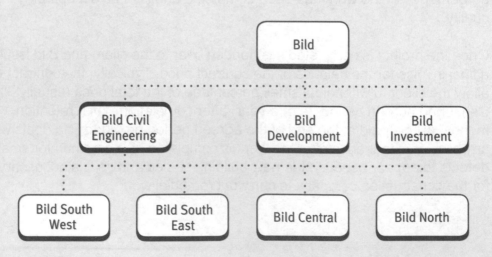

Bild's head office is in Capital City. Bild Civil Engineering, Bild Development and Bild Investment also operate out of the head office building.

Bild Civil Engineering's four regional subsidiaries have their own separate offices, each located in its respective region.

Each contract has a team of site agents who work out of temporary offices on the site. Their job is to supervise the subcontractors who undertake most of the actual physical work in terms of labour and providing construction equipment. The site agents also raise purchase orders for building materials. The materials are shipped directly to the site. The site agents are supported by architects, civil engineers, quantity surveyors and support staff at the subsidiary company's office.

The regional subsidiaries operate independently of each other. Each reports to Bild Civil Engineering on a half-yearly basis. Bild Civil Engineering consolidates the reports into a summary for Bild's main board to consider.

Bild's main board receives high-level reports summarising the key results of Bild Civil Engineering, Bild Development and Bild Investment.

Budget reports

The following is a typical budget report submitted by a regional subsidiary. Actual results are reported against budget for key performance targets. The regional CEO provides a brief commentary explaining why variances have arisen. Bild South West has historically been the most profitable regional subsidiary with results consistently in line with budgets.

Management report – Bild South West Six months to 31 March 2015		
	$m Budget	$m Actual
New work bid for	2,200	1,850
Contract won	765	530
Progress payments invoiced	760	730
Retention monies released	89	52
Cost of work scheduled (CWS)	831	963
Cost of work performed (CWP)	721	748
Schedule variance (CWP – CWS)	110A	
Cost variance (CWP – CWP)		27A

Commentary by Bild South West CEO

Results for the six months have been disappointing. In particular, we have had fewer opportunities to tender for work than we had originally anticipated. We also won just over 30% less work than budgeted. This will leave us with excess capacity for the next three months. We were successful at bidding for smaller contracts but Constructmore outbid us for two large projects, which was particularly disappointing because we have undertaken work for those clients in the past and they have been happy with the quality of our work. It appears that Constructmore undercut our bids for these contracts.

Stock market and corporate governance

Bild's share price has remained reasonably stable over the last three years, despite stiff competition. The share price is, however, currently at its lowest price in the company's history. The company has struggled to achieve the growth it hoped for.

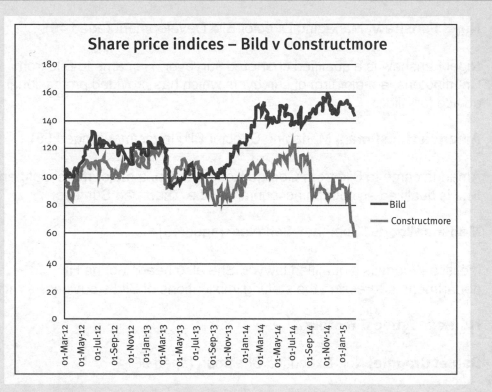

Share price indices – Bild v Constructmore

Market data

Bild's historical beta is 1.8

The equity market premium is 6%

The risk free rate is 5%

Bild's Board of Directors

Executive directors

Andrew Mitchell, Chief Executive Officer (aged 53)

Andrew Mitchell is a qualified civil engineer. He was formerly the Managing Director of Bild Civil Engineering. He joined Bild in 1994 and has led many successful construction projects.

Felicity Bunyan, Group Finance Director (aged 62)

Felicity Bunyan is a qualified accountant with extensive knowledge of the construction sector. She has worked for a variety of organisations including an engineering company based in Australia.

Mark Grassington, Managing Director Bild Civil Engineering (aged 47)

Mark Grassington joined Bild from a major competitor Constructmore in 2010. After working for the South East subsidiary, he successfully led a new "quality matters" initiative through all four regional subsidiaries before being promoted to Managing Director in 2013.

Nigel Fanshaw, Managing Director Bild Development (aged 49)

Nigel Fanshaw is a qualified chartered surveyor. He came to Bild from Chuffingtons, a major firm of surveyors which has provided professional advice for Bild.

Amanda Hessilman, Managing Director Bild Investment (aged 55)

Amanda came to Bild from George Hope and Co, a major merchant bank. She is qualified as both an accountant and a Chartered Surveyor.

Melissa Woods, Company Secretary (aged 46)

Melissa Woods is a qualified lawyer. She also heads up the HR department, addressing the staffing implications of Bild's business strategy.

Non-executive directors

Daniel Craggie, Non-Executive Chairman (aged 68)

Daniel Craggie came to Bild as a Non-Executive Director in 2010 and was appointed Chairman in 2012. He was previously Finance Director for another major company in the construction industry. He has had an illustrious career in the construction industry.

Jessie Hardbotham, Senior Independent Director (aged 65)

Jessie Hardbotham is also chair of the audit committee. She is a trustee of a major national charity following a successful career as an academic.

Nimrod Ekserdjian, Independent Non-Executive Director (aged 61)

Nimrod Ekserdjian is a member of the audit and remuneration committees. He has enjoyed a distinguished career in the public sector and is a former senior town planner.

Haofeng Liu, Independent Non-Executive Director (aged 58)

Haofeng Liu has held directorships for several international construction companies and is a specialist in sustainable development and environmentally friendly construction methodologies. He is chair of the remuneration committee.

Hugo Hunter, Independent Non-Executive Director (aged 47)

Hugo Hunter is Chairman of Hunter and Waddell, a prestigious property investment company. He is a member of the remuneration committee.

Reference material 2:

Extracts from financial statements – Bild

Bild GroupConsolidated statements of profit or loss

For the year ended 30 September 2014

	Notes	2014	2013
		$m	$m
Revenue	1	7,631	7,084
Cost of sales		–6,926	–6,382
Gross profit		705	702
Other net operating expense		–367	–312
Investment income		27	29
Finance expense		–54	–52
Profit before tax		311	367
Tax	4	–132	–129
Profit for the year		179	238

Bild Group – Consolidated statement of financial position as at 30 September 2014

	Notes	2014 $m	2013 $m
Non-current assets			
Intangible assets		240	240
Property plant and equipment	2	790	721
		1,030	961
Current assets			
Inventory		298	287
Due from construction clients		432	336
Trade receivables		23	15
Cash		19	67
Assets held for sale		43	62
		815	767
		1,845	1,728
Equity			
Share capital	3	240	240
Share premium		32	32
Revaluation reserve		165	165
Retained earnings		428	370
		865	807

Non-current liabilities

Provisions	128	112
Borrowings	426	414
Deferred tax	18	16
Retirement liabilities	137	135
	709	677

Current liabilities

Trade payables	21	41
Borrowings	235	190
Tax liability	15	13
	271	244
	1,845	1,728

Bild Group – Consolidated statement of changes in equity for the year ended 30 September 2014

	Share capital	Share premium	Revaluation reserve	Retained earnings	Total equity
	$m	$m	$m	$m	$m
Balance as at 1 October 2013	240	32	165	370	807
Profit of the year				179	179
Dividend paid				121	121
Balance as at 30 September 2014	240	32	165	428	865

Notes to the accounts

(1) Revenue	2014	2013
	$m	$m
Revenue from construction services	6,872	6,488
Proceeds from sale of developments	759	596
	7,631	7,084

(2) Property plant and equipment	$m
Cost or valuation	
At 1 October 2013	981
Additions	158
Disposals	105
Impairment	0
At 30 September 2014	1,034
Accumulated depreciation	
At 1 October 2013	260
Charge for the year	23
Disposals	39
At 30 September 2014	244
Carrying amount	790

The directors carried out a review of the values of property plant and equipment and did not find any evidence of impairment.

(3) Share Capital

Bild has issued share capital of 240million shares of $1.

At 31 September 2014 the share price was $3.50

(4) Taxation

The corporation tax rate in Ceeland is 35%

Reference material 3:

Accounting policies

Bild complies with IFRS.

Property plant and equipment

Property, plant and equipment comprises properties held for investment purposes, a land bank intended for future development and Bild's head office.

Property plant and equipment is held under the revaluation model in accordance with IAS 16. Items of property plant and equipment are carried at a revalued amount, being the fair value at the date of the revaluation less any subsequent accumulated depreciation. Reviews are carried out by the directors on an annual basis to ensure that the carrying amount does not differ materially from that which would be determined using fair value at the end of the reporting period. Every five years an independent valuation is carried out by a firm of professional surveyors and valuers. The next such review is due in 2017.

Leases

Leases on plant and equipment are classed as operating leases. Lease payments are recognised within cost of sales in the income statement.

Reference material 4:

Principal risks

Risk and impact	Mitigation
Failing to win contracts in existing and new target markets, leading to failure to achieve targets for revenue growth and profits.	Listening to our customers to ensure that we understand and meet their needs. Implementing cost reduction programmes to ensure that we remain competitive.
Problems with operational delivery, cost overruns, time overruns and design faults.	Work on site is checked by in house professionals and reports prepared so that any necessary corrective action can be taken. The Board is responsible for overall quality issues and reviewing best practice.
The success of the business is dependent upon sufficient financial facilities.	Cash forecasts are prepared regularly providing accurate information. Borrowing facilities have been successfully renegotiated and extended.
Bild's activities require the continuous monitoring of the management of health and safety risks. Failure to manage these risks could lead to injury to employees and subcontractors and could also expose Bild to legal liability and reputational damage.	We have detailed health and safety policies and procedures in place. These are reviewed and monitored by management.
The business depends on a flexible, skilled and well-motivated workforce. If we are not able to attract and retain skilled people then business growth may not be possible.	Staff turnover is monitored and pay and conditions are regularly reviewed against benchmarks to ensure that Bild remains competitive. Bild has a performance review process designed to assist the career development of staff.
Future construction orders depend on the economic climate and the availability of credit for private sector expenditure.	The Board carries out quarterly reviews of workload. Bild has a network of regional offices throughout Ceeland providing strong integration with our client base.

Reference material 5:

Extract from Chairman's statement

I am happy to report a very positive set of results for Bild for the year ended 30 September 2014.

Our core business of construction has remained profitable, despite erosion of margins. That profit has been supplemented by contributions from our property development subsidiary, including the successful sale of our major office development in Capital City. Bild Investment has also continued to provide positive returns.

In addition to valuable contributions to group revenue and profits, our investment and development activities also provide a solid asset base on which to secure borrowings. Our land bank and investment properties have shown steady growth in value. Our asset base, combined with our positive relationship with lenders, has enabled Bild to sustain gearing levels well in excess of our main competitors.

We are looking ahead to substantial opportunities in the marketplace, where we have already demonstrated we have the skills, experience and financial resources to compete and succeed. We have been successful in securing a number of new contracts and have also been able to extend some existing contracts. Our order book is almost at the same level as at September 2013, despite challenging economic conditions.

Daniel Craggie
Chairman

Reference material 6:

Extract from financial statements – Constructmore

Consolidated income statements For the year ended 30 September 2014

	2014	2013
	$m	$m
Revenue	9,743	9,898
Cost of Sales	−9,066	−9,212
Gross profit	677	686
Other net operating expenses	−253	−269
Investment income	0	0
Finance expense	−23	−19
Profit before tax	401	398
Tax	−165	−172
Profit for the year	236	226

Constructmore – Consolidated statement of financial position as at 30 September 2014

	2014	2013
	$m	$m
Non-current assets		
Intangible assets	730	798
Property, plant and equipment	125	109
	855	907
Current assets		
Inventory	220	189
Due from construction clients	480	413
Trade receivables	376	329
Cash	390	470
	1,466	1,401
	2,321	2,308
Equity		
Share capital	700	700
Share premium	160	160
Retained earnings	123	152
	983	1,012
Non-current liabilities		
Provisions	323	298
Borrowings	23	23
Deferred tax	74	62
Retirement liabilities	370	330
	790	713

Current liabilities

Trade payable	278	219
Borrowings	123	190
Tax	147	174
	548	583
	2,321	2,308

Key ratios

	2014	2013
Bild		
Gross profit %	9.2	9.9
Profit for year as a % of revenue	2.4	3.4
ROCE %	21.5	26.3
Gearing (D/D+E)	45	45.6
Constructmore		
Gross profit %	7.0	7.0
Profit for year as a % of revenue	2.4	2.3
ROCE %	23.9	24.2
Gearing (D/D+E)	44.5	41.3

Reference material 7

Summary Management Report for Bild Board

For six months to 31 March 2015

Results to date – revenue and profit

Actual against budget for six months to 31 March 2015

$million	Civil engineering		Development		Investment	
	budget	actual	budget	actual	budget	actual
Revenue	3,500	3,374	420	115	38	37
Gross profit	332	301	53	12	36	35
Net profit	36	33	39	8	34	33

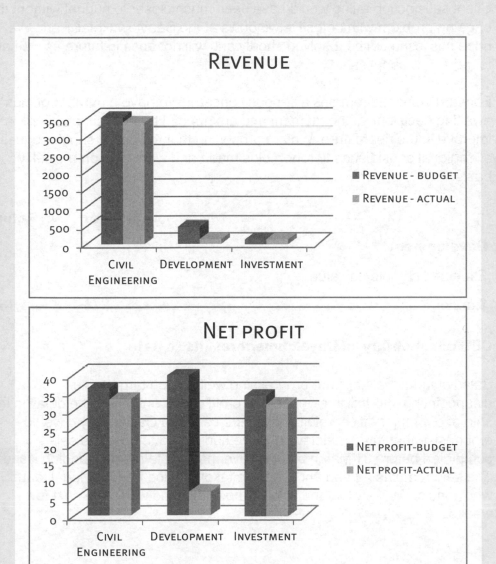

Key performance indicators and CEO commentary

	Budget	Actual
Civil Engineering		
Repeat business %	25	23
Client satisfaction %	95	83
Committed forward workload	2,700	1,560

CEO commentary on Civil Engineering results to date

Despite difficult economic conditions both revenue and profit are only just lower than an ambitious budget set for the first half of the year. We are delighted that the percentage of repeat business is holding up so well and only just below budget. 83% client satisfaction is a very high percentage. Client satisfaction rating would have been much closer to budget without the ongoing problem with defective windows at the Seaview Retail Park. We hope this issue will be resolved shortly and will not arise in future as we have found a new supplier.

Forward workload remains a serious concern. We have a number of bids awaiting decisions at the moment and are hopeful that the situation will improve in the near future. We are proposing that the board should request all regional subsidiaries to report bids made and work won on a weekly basis.

	Budget	Actual
Development		
Expected completed value		
$ million	1,278	1,180

CEO commentary on Development results to date

Sales of industrial units are progressing well and on target. The disappointing shortfall in revenue and profit is due entirely to the delay in the sale of our major office, retail and leisure centre in Capital City. I would emphasise that this is a delay only. We had aimed to have the sale completed before 31 March but the buyer has still to resolve funding issues. The sale remains agreed and we have taken advice from our legal team who consider it likely that the sale will be completed within the next few weeks.

	Budget	Actual
Investment		
Overall occupancy rate %	95	92
Average rent per sq meter $	250	247

CEO commentary on Investment results to date

The investment subsidiary continues to make steady and reliable returns on investment. Our occupancy rate, while below budget, is above that of similar investment companies, due largely to our high quality portfolio. Average rents are also holding up well and while in the current economic climate we have not always been able to negotiate increased rental levels when reviews are due, we have not been forced to reduce rents or to offer excessive rent free periods. Overall the performance to date has been good and this should continue for the rest of this financial year.

CONSTRUCTION NEWS

Reference material: 8

What does 2015 hold for the construction industry in Ceeland?

A report by our economics editor

4 January 2015

The construction industry in Ceeland is notoriously cyclical; activity is high when the economy is prosperous and low during downturns. So how does the economy look in 2015? Construction companies range from very small owner run building firms to major contractors. For this article we have focussed on those with a turnover in excess of $100m per annum. This gave us a sample of 63 companies, five fewer than last year's survey because one company has since gone into receivership and another four have had their revenues decline below $100m.

Although construction output increased, there are worrying signs that the rate of growth is slowing down. This may not be too damaging as there is also evidence of capacity constraints, with subcontractor availability falling sharply and steep increases in the demand for construction materials. It will always be a struggle to maintain activity levels because even the largest contractors find that their ongoing workload comprises a small number of very large contracts. The successful completion of a shopping mall or motorway extension leaves a void in the order book.

Construction companies tend to have low gearing levels; the average gearing ratio for our sample was 17%, with 12 of our companies having no net debt at all. Return on Capital Employed averaged 23%, but operating profit averaged only 1.5% of reported revenue.

Seven of our companies had a "company health score" that was low enough to cause concern that they may be financially vulnerable.

How many companies will we survey when we repeat this exercise next year? Steadily rising costs and downward pressure on prices in a highly competitive market may mean that even the largest will struggle to maintain their forward workload.

ECONOMICS TODAY

Reference material 8:

6 January 2015

PFI – the way forward for Ceeland?

The Private Finance Initiative (PFI) has been widely used in many countries as a procurement method to deliver public sector infrastructure projects. Recent announcements by the Ceeland Government indicate that following a successful series of pilot projects this type of finance is now to be used in Ceeland for the provision of new schools, hospitals and roads.

PFI comes under the broader term of PPP (Public Private Partnerships.) Under PFI, a private sector developer pays for the construction of a project on behalf of a public sector client. Once built, the developer leases the resulting school, hospital or whatever on a fully-serviced basis for an agreed period spanning the expected life of the buildings. So, the developer provides cleaning, catering and maintenance facilities while the public sector client pays the teachers or the medical staff and supplies the textbooks or the medicines. The companies offering this service claim that it provides an exciting new means of funding public sector services. Politicians are often attracted by the fact that they can improve public infrastructure without having to find the money up front.

Announcing the new initiative, a Ceeland Government spokesman stated "we hope that PFI will deliver new projects more quickly than the public sector acting alone, and at a lower risk. Although some countries have had problems with PFI initiatives, we believe that Ceeland can learn from others' mistakes to ensure that projects represent good value for money for Ceeland's taxpayers, while also providing high quality buildings and services."

The Government spokesman was questioned about the recent public inquiry in neighbouring county Deeland into the PFI project to build BigCity Hospital. The project suffered from major cost overruns because the building specification was constantly changed in response to new medical technologies that became available during the design and building phases of the project. There have also been public protests about the level of cleanliness in the hospital and the standard of food provided for patients. Protesters have claimed that these problems are attributable to the developer's incentive to minimise costs in order to maximise profits, even if doing so was at the expense of patient care.

The Ceeland Government spokesman insisted that the Government's PFI team had visited several projects in overseas countries, including the BigCity Hospital in Deeland. "Although this project has had problems, there have been many examples of highly successful projects. We remain confident that partnerships with the private sector can deliver high quality schools and hospitals in Ceeland."

March 2015 Exam – summary of the preseen

In Chapter Five we showed you some techniques to help you in your analysis of the pre-seen. Once you have completed your analysis of the pre-seen for the March 2015 sitting, BILD, you can review this chapter to ensure you have identified the key points. We will take you through each exhibit highlighting the key conclusions before bringing this together into a summary using the SWOT framework.

1 Exhibit by Exhibit Analysis

Reference material 1 – Company and background information

BILD – Company Background

Based in its home country of Ceeland, BILD is the third largest company in the construction industry sector. BILD's main competitor is Constructmore.

The company participates in three activities namely civil engineering, development and investment. All three activities are managed by separate subsidiary companies with civil engineering being the principal business. This would imply that BILD will need clear and accurate communication lines between these subsidiary companies to be sure of good operational control.

Civil engineering

BILD's principal activity is undertaking civil engineering projects to build offices, roads and infrastructure developments to include schools and hospitals for which it has a good reputation.

The fact that there are high levels of competition within the industry and contracts are subject to bidding procedures suggests that BILD will need to be competitive in their pricing but given the controls within the construction industry over health and safety and quality, this could produce a conflict of objectives

These contracts can either require BILD to construct according to client specifications or alternatively be commissioned to assist the client with the design work. To facilitate the latter, BILD has its own professional surveyors, civil engineers and available outside professionals (with whom it has good contacts) who can be recruited whenever required. This suggests that the recruitment and retention of high quality personnel is a critical factor and in addition, the necessity to have strong links with professional outsourcers will similarly be important to maintain.

Development

This activity entails BILD undertaking some speculative ventures buying land and/or building projects (e.g. offices) and then finding a buyer when the work is completed. The word "speculative" implies the risk of getting this activity wrong is high leaving BILD with potentially unsaleable properties and the consequential effects on cost and profits.

Investment

For its investment activities, BILD has a separate subsidiary which may have had property transferred to it by the development subsidiary if the latter cannot find a buyer for any completed building. These buildings are rented to third parties pending sale at a future date when market conditions are suitable.

Both the investment and development activities are subject to market conditions which by implication are outside the control of BILD, making them extremely risky ventures. The reference to "renting" does however open up another line of business. More detail will be needed to establish how these rents are set, paid and accounted for.

Typical civil engineering project

The client will specify the project detail in the bidding process which will normally entail inviting several construction companies to bid. The bid involves the preparation and submission of complex documentation which takes a great deal of time to prepare and can include any of the following options:

- the client commissioning the design element from its own personnel

- the client commissioning the design work from independent firms

- the design work being part of the project that is awarded to the construction company

BILD may decline from submitting a bid with the decision being influenced by existing work commitments and the forecasted profitability of the project. These are sensitive decisions as the typical project can take up to five years to complete and as a result will require BILD to have detailed and accurate internal information on capacity, costs, availability of staff etc. to be sure that accurate decisions can be made on the preparation and acceptance of bids. Incorrect decisions in this context can affect the credibility of BILD in the industry, by not completing projects on time or not accepting projects when they clearly should have thus affecting future revenue and profit.

If BILD is awarded the contract, a project team manager will be appointed with BILD's project manager in overall command of the project assisted by other professionals as and when required.

The construction work is carried out by specialist subcontractors who will be employed and paid by BILD. During the project, BILD is additionally responsible for the completion of the project on time, the quality of the subcontractors work completed, the purchase of required materials and any other costs associated with the project other than the purchase of the land. In addition, the project is subdivided into stages and is subject to periodic review by the client for quality. The successful completion of a stage will result in progress payments being made.

It is clear from this information that the control of a project is vital for BILD. This will entail all aspects of project management and this key area of the syllabus should be thoroughly revised. Given the industry norm of the client retaining a percentage of the total price (between 3-5%) and the expectation of additional remedial work, the focus on detailed planning for all projects is critical.

Ceeland

With the dollar ($) as the currency, BILD will be subject to foreign exchange risk on the purchase of materials if they are shipped in from another country. This may be of particular relevance given that Ceeland is stated as having "good international trading links".

The climate may well affect the completion of projects (further emphasising the need for detailed planning) given that the country is subject to a rainy season for four months of the year. Similarly the possibility if natural disasters, coinciding with climate change should not be ruled out.

Job description

The description indicates that the main driver of the role you are adopting for BILD i.e. performance measurement and decision making, places significant emphasis on the P2 and E2 syllabi.

Organisation and structure

The diagram reinforces the structure previously described with the additional information that the Civil Engineering subsidiary is further subdivided into four regional subsidiaries each of which are responsible for their geographical area and operate independently of each other, raising the possibility of transfer pricing and sharing of equipment and personnel between each of the regional subsidiaries. Each regional subsidiary reports to the BILD civil engineering board on a half yearly basis. This time scale seems far too long and more detail will be needed as to what information is supplied.

The main board of BILD also has representation from each of the main subsidiaries (CEO) which further emphasises the regional structure and the decentralised approach to management. This approach requires a detailed knowledge of the regions and the customers. As a consequence, Business, Leadership and People skills(particularly communication skills) are likely to be of major importance, largely drawn of course form the E2 and P2 syllabi.

Additionally each contract has a team of site agents, supported by professional and support staff, who are responsible for supervising the subcontractors, raising purchase orders for building materials delivered directly to site. This creates a potential weakness in control procedures given that management reporting for these regional subsidiaries only takes place twice per year.

Budget reports

Indicating the most profitable subsidiary for the civil engineering activity is the South West, the report for the six months to 30 March 2015 presents a cause for concern given that fewer opportunities have arisen to tender for work, less work has been won that budgeted for and, as a result, there is excess capacity for the next quarter. Similarly, despite the clients being satisfied with the work completed by BILD they have lost out to the biggest competitor on new bids with the decision being based apparently on price.

This will clearly lead to some significant decisions as to how to use labour and resources over this period, as well as perhaps revisiting the pricing strategy given the increased competition depicted. Profitability calculations, pricing methodology and revisions to costing approaches are likely areas for the forthcoming examination and will need to be revised thoroughly.

Stock market and corporate governance

Although stable over the last three years, the share price is at its lowest level in BILD's history and continues to find it difficult to achieve its planned growth.

There will be an effect on shareholder confidence in this context and it will up to the main board to reassure the investors to maintain the support it needs in this highly competitive industry.

Market data

Beta is the tendency of a security's returns to respond to swings in the market. A beta of 1 indicates that the security's price will move with the market; a beta of less than 1 means that the share will be less volatile than the market; a beta of greater than 1 indicates that the share's price will be more volatile than the market. For example, if a beta is 1.2, is theoretically 20% more volatile than the market. This indicates therefore that the risk associated with investing in BILD s high.

Although this is not in the syllabus for the Management Level, it is an indication of the need to understand the risk associated with differing industries. It would be useful to research the beta factors for the construction industry players in the UK to draw comparisons. For example in January 2015, Redrow in the UK were posting a beta factor of 1.4 .

Board of Directors

The Board comprises of an appropriate number of well qualified executive and non-executive directors with substantial relevant work experience. The only concern in terms of board composition is Jessie Hardbotham as senior independent Director as she seems to lack relevant skills and experience for the construction industry. There is no mention of a nominations committee and the consideration of both if these aspects could question the recruitment policy of BILD.

Reference material 2 – Extracts from financial statements for the year ended 30 September 2014

Ratio	2014	2013
Revenue growth	7.72%	–
Gross profit margin	9.2%	9.9%
Profit for year margin	2.4%	3.4%
Return on capital employed	21.5%	26.3%
Gearing	45%	45.6%
Current ratio	1:1:3	1:1:31
Quick ratio	1:1:9	1:1:96

Revenue increased to $7631m ($7084m) an increase of 7.72%. This was greater than Constructmore's revenue growth which actually decreased during the year to $9743m ($9898). This suggests that BILD is holding its own against significant competition and difficult trading conditions.

Cost of sales has increased $7631 ($7084) but remains the same as a percentage of revenue i.e. 91%. Gross profit remains fairly static with only a small increase of $3m between 2013 and 2014 although there has been a fall of .07% over the two years.

The big unknown in the statement of profit or loss is the "other net operating expense" category. There is insufficient detail to understand the make up of the number but there has been a significant increase of $55m over the year (17.6%) which will require further detail to understand.

At profit for the year we can see the effect of the increase in costs with a significant 25% decrease posted throughout the year from $238m in 2013 to $179m in 2014. Further detail on the costs incurred would be required to establish cause and effect of this change.

As would be expected from the above narrative, the decrease in profit and increase in costs have produced a fall in return on capital employed to 21.5% (26.3%).

The gearing figure highlights the level of debt that BILD is utilising to finance its activities. Generally something between 25% and 50% is considered normal although it does depend on circumstances and it should be remembered that any debt will carry with it a requirement to pay interest throughout the life of the debt. In theory, the higher the level of borrowing (gearing) the higher are the risks to a business, since the payment of interest and repayment of debts are not "optional" in the same way as dividends. However, gearing can be a financially sound part of a business's capital structure particularly if the business has strong, predictable cash flows.

The ability to raise further debt would depend upon their debt capacity, particularly its asset strength for providing security/collateral for the debts. Without any security the cost of unsecured debt borrowing is likely to be high.

According to the Statement of Financial Position, while BILD has just over $1.03 billion of non-current assets, only $790m of this is tangible, the remainder consisting of intangibles. We are not provided with the make-up of these intangibles.

The tangible non-current assets consist of property as well as plant and equipment. The plant and equipment is expanded on in note 2 which shows some significant activity in terms of additions and disposals throughout the year. Given the nature of the development and investment business, we should expect perhaps more detail in this aspect to follow.

Cash has decreased substantially to $19m ($67m) and the current ratio is quite low at 1:1.3 with very little movement throughout the year. The quick (liquidity) ratio is more satisfactory with BILD able to cover its short tern debts by a factor of 2.

Reference material 3 – Accounting policies

It is stated that property, plant and equipment (PPE) is held under the guidelines of IAS 16 with yearly internal reviews undertaken and independent valuations every five years to substantiate these claims. Similarly leases on plant and equipment are recognised within cost of sales. More information is required to determine if this is in line with accounting and industry standards which provides an opportunity for industry relevant industry research.

Reference material 4 – Principal risks

Failing to win contracts in existing and new target markets

This risk seems to link with the most recent information from the South West division budget report in that the budgeted amount of work has not been achieved. The mitigation suggested makes perfect sense but, based on the feedback from the South West division, clients are less than satisfied with the quality of some of BILD's work which would suggest more work needs to be done to establish the reasons for these opinions. New measures may need to be implemented bringing in more of an emphasis on a balanced scorecard approach from the P2 syllabus.

Problems with operational delivery

Clearly overruns on cost and time must be avoided and are two of the fundamental building bricks of good project management, critical to the success of BILD. The fact that the work is checked is good but we would need to assess the content and the quality of these reviews given the comments on quality for the South West customers already discussed above. Again new measures, revisions to performance criteria and the qualifications of those commissioned to carry out these reviews will need to be established.

Insufficient financial facilities

Key to success in the construction industry is cash. We are told that cash forecasts are prepared but they are not provided in the pre-seen information. Clearly this is an area of major concerns and as such it would be very sensible to revise this area and expect to see cash forecast (good or bad) presented to us in the real exam.

Health and safety

The construction industry is prone to accidents given the nature of the work which often dangerous, being carried out in difficult and challenging circumstances. The pre-seen suggests that BILD has detailed policies and procedures and we should expect these to be presented and perhaps challenged in the real exam. Health and safety and its management is contained within the E2 syllabus.

Retention and attraction of skilled personnel

The mention of staff turnover but the absence of any information as to the levels within BILD would suggest that this, along with performance reviews and pay and conditions could be an area of concern. Poor performance is this clearly sensitive area could well challenge the success of BILD and present reputational and recruitment problems.

Economic climate

Economic fluctuations are issues facing every business. There is little that can be done to prevent them but it is possible to build and maintain a good reputation with clients to generate brand loyalty. In this context BILD seem to be using its network to protect its reputation. Critical to the success of this network will be the quality of the communication and the manner in which regional managers are monitored and appraised.

Reference material 5 – Chairman's statement

The statement from the Chairman is typically optimistic but does indicate some serious concerns for BILD in terms of margin erosion for the core business of construction and a contradiction concerning the successful sale of the office development in Capital City. This contradiction concerns the delay in the sale of this development which is raised in the CEO commentary on half yearly results in reference material 7 (page 21).

In addition, there is further reference to the value of the asset base and the comparison of gearing levels with the main competitors. This does suggest that this may be brought into question in the real exam.

Further contradiction is noted when we consider the reference to the "securing of a number of new contracts" as in the budget report for South West region we are told that they have won some 30% less new work than was originally budgeted for.

The overall opinion having read this statement is of a Chairman who seems out of touch with the real events befalling the company. By implication the statement raises concerns over the quality of the information provided, the leadership of BILD and the decisions that will subsequently result. These are key topics within the three syllabus areas supporting the MCS examination and we should expect to see these thoroughly tested.

Reference material 6 – Extract from Constructmore's financial statements

Ratio	2014	2013
Revenue growth	(0.02%)	–
Gross profit margin	7.0%	7.0%
Profit for year margin	2.4%	2.3%
Return on capital employed	23.9%	24.2%
Gearing	44.5%	41.3%
Current ratio	1:2:68	1:2:40
Quick ratio	1:2:27	1:2:08

Revenue decreased during the year to $9743m ($9898). This confirms that BILD is holding its own against significant competition and difficult trading conditions.

Cost of sales has decreased $9066 ($9212), remaining the same as a percentage of revenue i.e. 93%. Gross profit remains static at 7.0% suggesting that Constructmore has good control over its material supply.

As with BILD the big unknown in the statement of profit or loss is the "other net operating expense" category. There is insufficient detail to understand the make up of the number but there has been a decrease of $16m over the year (6%) which will require further information and analysis to understand. It is likely therefore that more information will be presented to us in the real exam to facilitate further comparison. On the surface however given that BILD has increased the expense in this category and Constructmore decreased it can be assumed that the latter business has more control over its operating expenses.

Profit for the year demonstrates the effect of the decrease in costs and therefore good cost control with a 4% increase posted throughout the year from $226m in 2013 to $236m in 2014. Further detail on the costs incurred would be required to establish cause and effect of this change.

There has been a fall in return on capital employed of 23.9% (24.2%) which seems surprising given that profit before tax has increased. However a closer look at statement of financial position reveals that non-current assets have fallen over the year leaving only marginal increase in total asset value of $13m over the course of the year. This decrease has been brought about by a fall in intangible assets of which we are provided with no further detail.

The gearing figure has increased over the year to 44.5%. Whilst this is in no way catastrophic, it does highlight the level of debt that they are utilising to finance activities. Given that retained earnings have also decreased, causing equity levels to fall, it is intriguing to note and more detail maybe provided at a later date. Generally something between 25% and 50% is considered normal.

As with BILD, the ability to raise further debt would depend upon their debt capacity, particularly its asset strength for providing security/collateral for the debts. Without any security the cost of unsecured debt borrowing is likely to be high.

The current ratio and quick ratios are healthy suggesting good control over working capital.

Reference material 7 – BILD Summary Management report – six months to 31.03.2015

The information presented provides more up to date detail on the split of revenue, gross profit and net profit for the three activities of civil engineering, development and investment for the first six months of the current trading year.

Based on the information provided, BILD has endured even more loss of income failing against budgeted revenue in all three activities but in particular the core business of civil engineering. Gross profit and net profit have similarly suffered.

Given that Ceeland endures a rainy season between November and February each year, it is not unexpected that the civil engineering business may suffer setbacks in completion of works etc. Having said that most significant drops in revenue and profit are in the development activity from $420m budgeted to $115 actual, this may be attributable to the delayed sale of the office development in Capital City but we do not have any numbers to substantiate this assumption.

Civil engineering

The KPI's for civil engineering also reveal a steadily worsening situation with repeat business, client satisfaction and committed forward workload all failing to achieve budget. Particular concern should be paid to the latter figure which has fallen dramatically $2700 budget to $1560 actual. This seems to confirm the Chairman's statement of order book figures being at the 2013 level and despite his enthusiasm these are not encouraging numbers. The move to increase reporting of bids to weekly submissions merely adds to these concerns, raising doubt over the accuracy of the budgets and the true effect of the harsh trading conditions.

Development

The introduction of a new KPI i.e. expected completed value is confusing and is supported by no additional explanation as to where it is derived from or its significance as a KPI.

Further information is provided on the delay in the sale of the office development at Capital City as well as renewed attempts to view this as "only a delay" with the sale agreed. Contracts however do not appear to have been exchanged so given the involvement of the legal department this may be a serious issue affecting both the reputation and future growth prospects of BILD.

Investment

Occupancy rates are shown as being above similar investment companies, although no further information is supplied? Average rents are being maintained and overall this business appears to be doing well given the difficult trading conditions.

Overall summary

Within the organisation there seems to be a contradiction of opinion as to the severity of the situation within civil engineering and BILD clearly has problems with its core business.

These circumstances provide food for thought and key aspects of the manner in which BILD is managed are challenged by these circumstances. For example:

- The accuracy of the costing methods
- The relevance of the performance measures
- If the situation continues or worsens, what will be the effect on stakeholders, the financial support they offer and ultimately the share price?

These represent key syllabus areas within CIMA's Operational and Management levels and will need to be thoroughly revised.

Reference material 8 – Construction News Article

The article serves to cement (excuse the pun) many of the messages already provided in the pre-seen.

For example:

- BILD's susceptibility to fluctuating economic conditions

- Over commitment to very large projects and therefore constraints on capacity

- Rising costs, increased pressure on prices that are acceptable to clients

An additional piece of information provides some further evidence on the key financial measure we have already discussed. Whilst ROCE is comparable to industry norms for the sample tested, gearing levels for BILD and Constructmore are significantly higher. This will of course affect the cost of debt and ultimately the calculation of WACC – is this an indicator from the examiner that long term finance and cost of capital will be examined? They are both of course key F2 topics.

Reference material 9 – Article from Economics Today

The PFI approach to financing key infrastructure projects is to be used in Ceeland.

Given the problems noted above and the potential effect on future contracts, this may provide BILD with an ideal opportunity for future growth. As such the evaluation of these options, the change to strategic direction and the management of these new approaches are likely to be key topics in the forthcoming exam.

2 SWOT analysis

A SWOT analysis is a useful tool to summarise the current position of the company. It is simply a listing of the following:

- The STRENGTHS of the organisation. These are internal factors that give the organisation a distinct advantage.

- The WEAKNESSES of the organisation. These are internal factors that affect performance adversely, and so might put the organisation at a disadvantage.

- The OPPORTUNITIES available. These are circumstances or developments in the environment that the organisation might be in a position to exploit to its advantage.

- The THREATS or potential threats. These are factors in the environment that present risks or potential risks to the organisation and its competitive position.

Strengths and weaknesses are internal to the organisation, whereas opportunities and threats result from the effect of external factors.

A SWOT analysis can be presented simply as a list of strengths, followed by weaknesses, then opportunities and finally threats. It would be useful to indicate within each category which factors seem more significant than others, perhaps by listing them in descending order of priority.

Alternatively a SWOT analysis, if it is not too long and excludes minor factors, can be presented in the form of a 2 × 2 table, as follows:

Strengths	Weaknesses
Opportunities	Threats

With this method of presentation, the positive factors (strengths and opportunities) are listed on the left and the negative factors (weaknesses and threats) are on the right.

Exercise – 1 SWOT analysis

Prepare a SWOT analysis of BILD based on the summary of each exhibit and the guidance above

Test your understanding answers

Exercise – 1 SWOT analysis

Strengths	Weaknesses
• Market share	• Speculative investments
• Customer relationships	• Bid preparation
• Range of activities	• Over capacity
• Good reputation	• Reporting timescales – subsidiaries
• High quality personnel	• Material purchase controls
• Rental income	• NED experience
• Revenue growth	• Cost of sales increase
• Customer knowledge	• Other expense increase
• Asset base	• Falling cash balance
	• Valuation of assets timescale
	• Retention of personnel
	• Optimistic Chairman

Opportunities	Threats
• Expansion of rental business	• Competition intense
• Sale of investment property	• Rising costs
• Acquisition of similar companies	• Pressure on pricing by clients
• New product innovation	• Economic climate
• Expansion in different market	• Foreign currency risk
• PFI/PPP	• Climatic conditions
	• Declining work opportunities
	• Low and falling share price
	• Failing to complete project on time
	• Health and safety
	• Lost income in civil engineering
	• Client satisfaction falling
	• Forward workload falling against budget
	• Office development sale

March 2015 Exam variant 5 – unseen information

Management Level Case Study Exam

This examination is structured as follows:

Section number	Number of tasks	Time for section (minutes)
1	1	45
2	1	45
3	1	45
4	1	45

The time available for each section is for reading, writing and planning your answer(s).

This information will be available for you to access during the examination by clicking on the Pre-seen button

Section 1

You have just received the following email:

> From: Felicity Bunyan, Group Finance Director
>
> To: Senior Management Accountant
>
> **Subject: commercial training**
>
> Hi,
>
> The non-executive directors have suggested that they would benefit from some formal training on the commercial background to our operations. They feel that they will be more effective if they have a better understanding of the issues that concern the board. The Chairman feels that the non-executive directors have been unwilling to express a view on many issues because they do not understand enough about the decisions that are being taken.
>
> I would like you to prepare a briefing document that the non-executives can read and then you can meet with the non-executives to discuss what you have said in your document.
>
> Your briefing document should cover two main issues:
>
> - What are the principal risks that affect Bild's ability to generate revenue?. You should focus on risks that are high impact and have a realistic probability of occurring.
>
> - What are the major challenges associated with developing and implementing a management strategy for Bild?
>
> Felicity

Requirement 1

Write your briefing document in the box below.

Section 2

You meet the Group Finance Director, Felicity Bunyan, in the corridor, where she tells you the following:

I am glad that I have bumped into you. Your discussion with the non-executive directors has encouraged them to take a more active interest in the workings of the company. To be honest, that is causing some resentment on the part of the executive directors, who feel that the non-executives are beginning to exceed their authority and to undermine the executive directors' management of the company.

I need you to write a briefing paper that would help us to resolve this concern without curbing the enthusiasm of the non-executives.

I think that you should cover the following areas:

- How can we ensure clear and effective communication between the executive and non-executive directors?

- How can we motivate the executive directors to make the best possible use of the non-executives' contribution?

- How can we manage the changing roles of executives and non-executive directors?

e.g

Requirement 2

Write your response to Felicity Bunyan's request in the box below.

```
```

e.g

Section 3

The following email has just arrived:

From: Felicity Bunyan, Group Finance Director

To: Senior Management Accountant

Subject: transfer pricing

I need your advice on a problem that has arisen over the past few months. Bild Civil Engineering's subsidiaries tend to hire construction plant and equipment, but own the more common items such as diggers and dumper trucks.

An internal audit investigation shows that subsidiaries have been hiring equipment from third parties that could have been borrowed from fellow subsidiaries. The reason for this has been that the hire charges have been lower than the internal transfer prices between subsidiaries. This is clearly dysfunctional behaviour and yet is difficult to address because of the huge variety of items that are owned and hired. It is not always clear to managers at head office that this is happening. At present we encourage subsidiary managers to negotiate a mutually agreeable transfer price however this has caused some dysfunctional behaviour. The other option is that the Finance Director from Head Office will set the transfer prices.

I would like you to draft a briefing paper for the board that deals with two issues:

- What are the difficulties associated with the two options?
- Which option will reduce the dysfunctional behavior, explaining how this will help to resolve any conflicts.

e.g

Requirement 3

Write your response to Felicity Bunyan's request in the box below.

e.g

You have received the following email:

From: Felicity Bunyan, Group Finance Director

To: Senior Management Accountant

Subject: tax management

We have had a very interesting proposal from a consulting firm (see below) that promises to reduce our tax expense quite considerably.

I would like you to consider this proposal and write a report covering:

- the potential effectiveness of this arrangement from a tax management point of view
- the impact of this arrangement on our market environment.

To: Felicity Bunyan

From: Consulting firm

Subject: tax management

Thank you for meeting with us today. We attach a summary of our suggested course of action. We propose to help you establish an overseas subsidiary ("Bild Procurement") in a country that has a favourable tax regime. The role of this company would be to act as a central buyer for all materials that are presently purchased by your regional civil engineering subsidiaries.

The system would operate as follows. The project management team would order materials as before, but would use Bild Procurement as the buyer. The goods would be delivered to the construction site in the same manner as before and without any delay, but Bild Procurement would resell the goods to the subsidiary, recognising a profit in the process.

All transactions would be priced in $ and Bild would have no exposure to foreign currency risk. Bild would, however, pay less tax because profit that would otherwise be reported and taxed in Bild's home country will now be taxed at a lower rate in Bild Procurement's home where the rate is lower.

It wouldn't even be necessary to establish a physical location or employ any staff overseas. Our associates would be able to provide a registered office and banking facilities for a normal fee.

Requirement 4

Write your response to Felicity Bunyan's request in the box below.

March 2015 Exam variant 5 – walkthrough of the unseen

Chapter learning objectives

- To gain further experience and develop exam technique by walking through and attempting another case study exam.

1 The Aim of a Walkthrough

The aim of this chapter is to give you a chance to practise many of the techniques you have been shown in previous chapters of this study text. This should help you to understand the various thought processes needed to complete the full three hour examination. It is important that you work through this chapter at a steady pace.

Don't rush on to the next stage until you have properly digested the information, followed the guidance labelled 'Stop and Think!' and made your own notes. This will give you more confidence than simply reading the model solutions. You should refer to the unseen produced in the previous chapter as you proceed through these exercises.

The following chapter will then guide you through the suggested solutions and marking key.

2 Summary of trigger and task 1

You have received an email from the Group Finance Director suggesting that the non-executive directors would benefit from some formal training on the commercial background to BILD's operations and in particular the issues that concern the board.

You have been requested to produce a briefing document for the non-executive directors to read in advance of a meeting which you will attend to discuss the contents of the document.

Stop and think!

(1) What do we know about BILD and the commercial challenges which face the business?

(2) Of those challenges, which ones are priorities for the board?

(3) What is the relevant information in the pre-seen? It's very important that your responses are applied to the scenario

3 Overview of task 1

You are required to prepare a briefing document which contains the following:

- The principal risks affecting BILD's ability to generate revenue

- The impact and probability of these risks occurring

- Major challenges when developing and implementing a management strategy.

Let's plan

We need to create a planning page that ensures you identify and respond to all parts of the requirement. You can use the techniques discussed in Chapter eight or develop your own method. In this chapter we will use the ordered list approach.

Split your planning sheet (use your wipe clean whiteboard) in two - one half for each part of the task, and then split the second section down further as follows.

You now need to brainstorm all the relevant points you can think of under the above headings, making sure you are bringing together your knowledge from the relevant syllabus as well as your analysis of the pre-seen information.

(NB Note that we have split the requirement into two parts as we are assuming that the first requirement is roughly the same size as the second and therefore each main task heading is equally weighted.)

Let's break down the requirements and consider all the key phrases to try and understand what the examiner is looking for. Remember that a failure to answer the question set is a key reason for failing the case study exam so be careful!

So the question is asking for "principal risks" which are provided in the preseen but then refining this to those affecting "revenue generation" with a "high impact" and a "realistic probability" of occurring. This requires the candidate to refine their selection of the risks they wish to include, therefore demonstrating the application of the syllabus and the preseen information. When you are trying to think of risks the best approach is to take a step back and think 'what could go wrong'. This should give you plenty of ideas.

The second part of the requirement focuses on two separate stages in the creation of a management strategy – i.e. the development stage and the implementation stage. This is a very practical question and as such will require a very practical approach, applying your response to risks identified in the first part of the question.

The principal risks affecting revenue generation

- Refer to the preseen information re principal risks facing BILD
- Refer to E2/P2 knowledge what is meant by "impact"
- Which of these risks have a "realistic probability" of occurring?
- What is likely to be the impact and how will affect BILD?

> **Major challenges when developing and implementing a management strategy**
>
> **Developing**
>
> - People and appropriate skills
> - External environment scanning and sources e.g. competitors, economic climate changes
>
> **Implementing**
>
> - Information sources
> - Communication in a complex structure
> - Leadership

As a rough rule of thumb you should spend about 15-20% of the time available for reading and planning. So for this section of the exam, where you are given 45 minutes, you should be spending approximately 8 minutes planning your answer before you complete the exercise below. This would leave you about 35 minutes to write your answer and a few minutes spare to check through what you have written.

Exercise – 1

Prepare a response to the first task in this variant of BILD.

4 Summary of trigger 2

In this section you are presented with a single document containing the trigger and task. We have considered the trigger and task elements together for consistency.

The board have been impressed with the feedback from the discussion that you have with the non-executive directors but are concerned now that the executive directors are becoming resentful as to the renewed vigour of the input from the non-executive directors which they feel is undermining their authority. The Group Finance Director (GFD) is concerned about this and wishes you to consider how to improve the communication between the executive and non-executive directors as well as motivating the former given the changing roles of each category of director.

Stop and think!

- Think about what the GFD is trying to achieve

- Consider who is responsible for effective (getting the job done) communication between the executive and non- executive directors.

- Consider the changing roles of the directors and the importance for BILD

5 Summary of task 2

You are asked to prepare a paper covering the following:

- How to ensure effective communication between the executive directors and non-executive directors?

- How to motivate the executive directors to utilise the non-executive contribution effectively?

- How to manage the changing roles of executive and non-executive directors?

Let's plan

Set up your whiteboard with three sections to begin with as the examiner presented the requirements for this task as three bullet points.

Effective communication between the executive directors and non-executive directors?
How to motivate the executive directors to utilise the non-executive contribution effectively?

> The changing roles of executive and non-executive directors?

Let's plan

You can use the method of planning shown above or refer to Chapter 8 and use a mind map instead. The important thing is to generate some ideas and get the main points in some order before you start to write.

When you are discussing communication, think about how it might work at BILD rather than simply listing ways the syllabus on effective communication. Start by thinking about the different ways that communication can be effective for board members and then, for each, discuss how useful this might be in BILD. There are 45 minutes in total for task 2, so you really need to address a range of specific methods rather than keeping your answer more generic.

For the second aspect it is vital that you can remember the basic ideas of motivation and how this might apply in the context of the relationship between executive and non-executive directors i.e. the former must be able to determine the benefit if the latter to be able to accept their views.

Now spend 8 minutes completing your plan before attempting Exercise 2. You would then have approximately 8 minutes to write your answer and a few minutes to check through what you have written before reviewing the solution.

Exercise – 2

Prepare a response to the second task in this variant of BILD

6 Summary of trigger 3

You receive an email from the Group Finance Director (GFD) expressing concerns surrounding the hiring of equipment from external sources at a cost which could have been avoided by borrowing the equipment from some of the other subsidiaries. This concern has arisen as a result of an internal audit report which has identified that the internal transfer prices between subsidiaries is higher than the external hire charge.

The GFD is alarmed at this dysfunctional behaviour and has asked for your opinion on two options put forward to correct the situation, namely to encourage negotiation between divisional managers to set an acceptable transfer price or to have the transfer price set centrally by Head Office.

Stop and think!

(1) What options are there available for the setting of the transfer price?

(2) How would these apply to BILD?

(3) How could either option assist in settling conflict between subsidiaries?

7 Summary of task 3

This task requires a discussion of:

* The difficulties associated with two transfer pricing options

* Which option will reduce any internal dysfunctional behaviour?

* How the chosen option will resolve any existing conflict?

Let's plan

Remember that you are aiming to get your main thoughts down with some kind of structure, ensuring you address all parts of the requirement. You are required to consider the difficulties associated with transfer pricing options and the effect of the selected option on dysfunctional behaviour. Your answer must consider the issues involved and focus on actions BILD can take and the benefits that may result in terms of conflict resolution.

Give yourself about 8 minutes to plan and then you can attempt exercise 3. You will then have approximately 35 minutes to write your answer, leaving a short amount of time to check through what you have written.

Exercise – 3

Prepare a response to the third task in this variant of BILD

8 Summary of trigger 4

You receive an email from the Group Finance Director (GFD) concerning a proposal from a consulting firm which could potentially reduce BILD's tax liability.

The proposal is to establish an overseas subsidiary (BILD Procurement) in a favourable tax regime with that subsidiary acting as a central buyer for all purchases of materials for the regional civil engineering subsidiaries. BILD Procurement would buy all the materials, resell them to the civil engineering subsidiaries with no effect on delivery, staff issues in the new subsidiary and no exposure to foreign currency risk.

The GFD has asked you to prepare a report which evaluates this proposal.

9 Summary of task 4

This task requires a discussion of:

- The effectiveness of the proposal from a tax management perspective.
- The impact of the proposal on BILD's market environment.

Let's plan

Remember that you are aiming to get your main thoughts down with some kind of structure, ensuring you address all parts of the requirement. You are required to consider the effectiveness of the proposal and the impact of the proposal on BILD's market environment. Your answer must consider the issues involved and focus on the tax management perspective as well as the external effect of BILD's actions should the proposal be accepted and implemented.

Give yourself about 8 minutes to plan and then you can attempt exercise 3. You will then have approximately 35 minutes to write your answer, leaving a short amount of time to check through what you have written.

Exercise – 4
Prepare a response to the third task in this variant of BILD

Test your understanding answers

Exercise – 1

Part (a)

Economic climate

Future construction orders depend on the economic climate and the availability of credit for private sector expenditure. The market is very competitive and a number of companies are chasing the same contracts, causing downward pressure on prices. Although Bild can strive to remain competitive, the economic climate and availability of private sector finance are out with their control.

Reputation risk

Bild is very dependent on a good reputation in order to generate future revenue. In a competitive market clients will not select a builder with a poor reputation. Any problems with cost overruns, time overruns or poor build quality would lead to loss of future business with that client. Publicity given to such problems would also potentially lose revenue with future clients. Problems on site may not be within Bild's control.

Staffing risk

Bild is dependent on the recruitment and retention of good quality, highly motivated staff in order to generate revenue. This is linked to reputation risk, for example problems with staff motivation could lead to build quality issues, completing projects on time may require staff to work extensive overtime. A significant proportion of Bild's revenue comes from repeat business and retaining key staff who have a good relationship with clients will be important for revenue generation.

Financial facilities

Bild cannot generate future revenue unless they have sufficient financial facilities. Construction clients pay in stages but do not pay for work in advance; Bild must have the resources needed to finance work in progress. Bild Development makes a significant contribution to revenue and profit but also requires significant cash investment. Accurate cash flow forecasting is therefore necessary but may be difficult due to the complexity of the business and the level of uncertainty caused by issues outside Bild's control (e.g. weather, construction start dates, development sale dates)

Part (b)

Challenges associated with developing and implementing a management strategy

Hiring and retaining the right people

This is a challenge for the board, particularly given the cyclical nature of the construction industry. When the market is buoyant, there will be a shortage of skilled construction workers and managers. When the market is in decline, difficult decisions will have to be made about which staff to retain, and which to make redundant.

Strategic planning

The market is challenging and evolving, for example PPP opportunities may now be available to Bild. The board need to examine trends and innovations and evaluate how to differentiate themselves from competitors and how client behaviours are changing.

Succession planning

The board need to develop future managers with leadership and business skills. For example project managers may have solid technical knowledge and leadership skills, but may also need to understand the financial impact of their actions, and be able to forecast cash flows accurately. Developing and promoting the best managers will help build a culture of long term client relationships.

Organisational structure

Bild is a complex organisation. Offices are located throughout Ceeland, projects vary from small units to very large ones and the management skills needed for civil engineering, development and investment are different. The board need to build a sustainable organisation and minimise dysfunctional decision making.

Exercise – 2

Part (a)

How can we ensure clear and effective communication between the executive and the non-executive directors?

Ensuring effective communication between exec and non-exec directors should be part of the role of the chairman. So the appointment of a strong chair, and making this part of his job description, should help.

It will be difficult for the non-execs to communicate effectively with executive directors if we do not have an induction program for executive and non-executive directors alike.

When the non- executive directors are appointed it should be clear what time commitment they are expected to give.

By ensuring the right people are appointed as non-executive directors who have useful experience, communication should be straightforward. By having diversity on the Board with the right mix of skills and experience this will facilitate good communication.

It is very important that all directors are given adequate information on Board proposals in a timely manner and of good quality. This is also part of the Chairman's role to ensure an agenda and information are communicated to the executive and non-executive directors. This is not simply a matter of making sure that reports are circulated in advance of board meetings. The information should be clear to all directors whatever their skills and expertise. The board needs information analysed in an insightful manner if it is to communicate effectively. The crucial relationship is that between the specialist directors, such as finance director, marketing director, chief executive and chairman. The finance director's duty is to give the board their own best judgement of Bild's financial position, but also to ensure that the financial information presented to the board has an appropriate level of detail and is understandable to directors who do not have an accounting qualification. This would apply to all discussions in any discipline: marketing, strategy, HR etc. This should help to facilitate the clarity and effectiveness of communication between directors.

Part (b)

There is a danger that executive directors see the role of non-executives as a "box ticking" exercise. A balanced board is a requirement but they may see no genuine benefit from the presence of non-execs. Since the training exercise for non-executives was a success, it may be worth carrying out similar training for executive directors so that they can better understand the role and benefits of the non-execs. This training could emphasise the benefits of the expertise that non execs bring to Bild. It could be carried out regularly, perhaps annually, to ensure that directors are aware of the changing roles.

An induction package should be an essential part of the introduction of all new directors to the company. The Company Secretary or other senior officer should discuss many of the duties that the directors will be expected to perform, introduce them to all the people they will be working with and answer any questions the new director has.

In order to motivate the exec directors it may also be necessary for them to see for themselves the benefit of the non-execs. Telling them that there are benefits may not be enough. The improvements in communication set out above should assist – if the directors are communicating effectively the benefits of the non-execs should be readily apparent. Again, it is important that the non-execs have credibility with the exec directors, and therefore recruitment of individuals with appropriate experience, good business judgement and integrity is vital.

The non-execs themselves also have some responsibility here, as part of their role is to challenge the executive board and perhaps present views which are not held by the majority of board members. Tact and diplomacy are important attributes for a non-exec. Again, the role of the chairman is important here; at the end of the day the board is just a committee and the chair has a responsibility to ensure that meetings are effective.

Exercise – 3

Part (a)

The most obvious solution is to set transfer prices below the prices charged by third parties. However, while this may encourage divisional managers to borrow from other divisions, it is unlikely to be sufficient to solve the problem.

Equipment hire prices are likely to fluctuate considerably. They are also likely to vary widely from location to location. If there is little construction activity in a given area on a particular week, it is likely that any equipment required could be borrowed cheaply. It would therefore be necessary to either re-set transfer prices very frequently, or to require divisions to undercut any hire quote received from outwith the Bild group. The process of obtaining an external hire quotation, and then asking for an internal bid against it, could be too cumbersome.

It might be possible to set transfer prices very low, so as to just cover any incremental costs incurred by the lender. This would encourage managers to borrow internally but might make them less willing to lend. The incremental costs arising from hiring are likely to be low.

One way to encourage divisional managers to borrow equipment in house would be to make this part of a balanced scorecard appraisal.

Another method might be to make internal hire very easy. An internal database could be set up showing what surplus equipment is held at each location, making it a straightforward exercise for managers to find what they need.

Part (b)

It is worth noting that Bild will tend to hire large items of plant for prolonged periods. That means that the cost of each hire contract will be potentially substantial and so it would be worth investing time and effort in its control.

Bild Civil Engineering should establish a plant hire department that authorises all hire contracts costing more than, say, $10,000. The department should be staffed by people with some understanding of the construction industry, so that they can understand the role of each item of equipment being hired.

Every request for authorisation should be accompanied by a document that identifies the contract, the location of the site and the nature of the work that must be undertaken. The plant hire department should be responsible for placing any orders for hire so that the regional subsidiaries do not simply hire from third parties as a matter of course.

The plant hire department should first check whether the item requested is in Bild's asset register. The asset register should contain a data field that makes it possible to search for, say, earth moving equipment. The asset register should indicate the location of the equipment and whether it is available for use or whether it is required for another contract. These would be further fields that would not normally be found on a typical asset register.

In deciding whether to use an asset belonging to a fellow division, the plant hire department should take account of the cost of transporting the asset to and from the site.

The plant hire department should estimate the cost of hiring the equipment commercially and should process an internal charge that is based on this market price whenever an asset is to be hired from a fellow division. That should ensure that both companies are willing to accept this arrangement because the owner is receiving a commercial rate and the hirer is not paying any more than would have been charged by a third party.

The plant hire department should also be analysing external hires to determine whether there are any assets that should be bought outright rather than hiring them. Having a central record of hires will alert the company to the fact that certain items of equipment are hired so frequently that it would be cheaper to buy them instead.

Exercise – 4

Part (a)

This scheme is unlikely to be successful.

Tax rates vary globally, and Ceeland's rate of 35% is relatively high. Many schemes exist where international companies seek to establish subsidiaries in the most advantageous tax locations. For example Starbucks sources its coffee from a wholesale trading subsidiary based in Switzerland which has a 12% tax rate on trading profits.

But Bild is not an international corporate; all its activities are based in Ceeland. Starbucks can argue that it makes economic sense to have one specialist coffee buying team to supply all Starbucks branches, wherever they are located in the world.. Bild cannot make a similar case for overseas sourcing of construction materials.

For the scheme to be successful, Bild procurement would have to buy construction materials at market prices and then sell them on to Bild at an inflated transfer price. This would lead to profits being located in Bild Procurement's low tax jurisdiction country.

The Ceeland tax authorities will challenge the arrangement unless Bild can demonstrate that the price paid to Bild Procurement is a fair market price. Indeed, with a tax rate of 35% the Ceeland tax authorities are likely to have considerable experience of investigating international tax avoidance schemes. Prices of construction materials are easily established and although Bild Procurement could probably justify an administration charge on top of market price, this is not going to be sufficient to shift profits to a lower tax jurisdiction. The promoters of the scheme are offering to have materials delivered to sites with no delay. The materials will therefore be sourced in Ceeland This, combined with the fact that Bild will pay prices set in $, and not have a physical office, or staff based overseas, will make it impossible to argue that this is not an artificial transaction designed purely to avoid tax.

Part (b)

Bild is under pressure to cut costs in order to remain competitive. Tax paid is one of those costs. Reducing the effective tax rate should, in theory, make Bild more competitive.

There is, however, the danger of reputational damage from this move. This may not affect Bild's entire client base; some clients may wish to source construction as cheaply as possible and not be interested in the tax arrangements of the builder.

On the other hand, Bild also does business with the public sector in Ceeland. For example there may be new PPP opportunities for Bild to carry out work in partnership with the Ceeland Government. It is less likely that the government would be willing to enter into a partnership with a company which is deliberately setting out to exploit tax loopholes in order to avoid paying tax in Ceeland.

Other companies have suffered reputational damage and loss of revenue when such arrangements have been made public. For example in the UK, Starbucks and Amazon have been subject to extensive detrimental publicity. The construction industry in Ceeland is highly competitive and Bild is the third largest participant. It is therefore likely that Bild's competitors would quickly notice this action by Bild and would act to ensure that it was well-publicised.

If, as seems likely, the attempt to reduce tax in this way were to prove unsuccessful, Bild would face both a failed tax avoidance scheme (with associated costs) and negative publicity.

16

March 2015 Exam variant 5 – debrief of marking guide

Chapter learning objectives

*   To gain a deeper understanding of how to write an answer that scores well in the real exam.

1 Introduction

As we have already explained in previous chapters the case study examinations are marked against a series of competencies. It is important that you understand this process to ensure you maximise your marks in the exam.

Once you have reviewed Chapter Fifteen, attempted the exercises and reviewed the suggested solutions, this chapter takes you through the detail of how these exercises would be marked.

2 Marking Guide

Section	Technical skills		Business Skills		People Skills		Leadership Skills		Inte-gration	Total
1	Risks affecting revenue	12	Management Strategy	11					2	25
2					Communication	8	Motivation	15	2	25
3	Control of hiring	14			Negotiation of transfer prices	10			1	25
4	Tax, pricing	12	Reput-ation	12					1	25
		38		23		18		15	6	100

3 Examiner's comments on the exam as a whole

After each sitting the examiners release their views and thoughts on the exam. This is what the examiner commented on the March 2015 exam as a whole (i.e. not related to a specific variant)

"In general there were some very short answers to the management case study. Candidates were not well prepared and did not seem to know much about the industry or the company. Given that the pre-seen material had been available for several weeks prior to the exam, this was disappointing.

Some candidates demonstrated a very poor understanding of several syllabus areas, including 'core' material of fundamental importance.

There was a tendency to summarise study material without relating it to the question, which is always unlikely to score highly.

Candidates must make better use of the opportunity to gain familiarity with the pre-seen material. It is unnecessary to memorise the material or to become an expert in the industry, but candidates should develop an understanding of the business.

Questions give explicit instructions as to what is to be provided and marks will not be awarded for anything that has not been requested. In particular, essays on the theory underlying the problem are unlikely to score well if the question asks for a response to a particular issue arising from a scenario.

With the time constraints in place candidates can only spend specific time on a task, therefore it is essential that candidates write the important points early in their answer before they run out of time."

4 Exam Task 1

Review of marking guide

The part of the marking guide that relates to this task is as follows:

Section	Technical skills		Business Skills		People Skills	Leadership Skills	Integration	Total
1	Risks affecting revenue	12	Management Strategy	11			2	25

It is always worth reviewing marking guides to check that you are happy with how you have answered the question, understand how the total marks have been allocated and how the different tasks relate to the competencies.

- The first section had a time allocation of 45 minutes, so was worth 25% of the marks

- Advising the board as to the principal risks is a technical aspect of the P2 syllabus, so earns technical skills marks

- Identifying strategic challenges and the problems in developing and implementing a management strategy calls upon linking the theory with the effect on BILD and hence will be awarded the business skills marks. During the exam however, the key focus should be on answering the question rather than attempting to which competency is being tested.

Task 1

Examiner's comments

The examiner's specific comments on task 1 were as follows:

"Both parts of this question deal with the training of non-executive directors on issues that will affect their ability to provide a useful service to the company. Both parts would reward an appreciation of the contents of the pre-seen material.

The first part asks about the principal risks that will affect the entity's ability to generate revenues. This discussion has to focus on risks that are <u>high probability and high impact</u>. The second part focuses on advising the board on the <u>challenges associated</u> with managing Bild's strategy"

If we link these comments to the general comments above, it becomes very clear that the students did not prepare well for this exam and did not seem to know much about the industry or the company.

Understanding the model answer

The first part of the task related to stating those risks of a high probability and high impact that would have an effect on BILD's ability to generate revenue. We can then list the risks and rank different alternatives. Once this has been achieved, it would be important to justify why you had made the selection, provide examples from the preseen where relevant and note any action that BILD may take to mitigate the effect of such risks.

The second part of the task provided a clear structure for the answer i.e. those challenges associated with <u>developing and implementing</u> a management strategy. It would be critical here to relate the answer to the preseen information which provided lots of clues in this respect.

Given this we can see that the model answer is structured as follows:

Part (a)

Economic climate

- dependency on the economic climate

- availability of credit for private sector expenditure.

- competitive nature of the market, the number of companies chasing the same contracts,

- the economic climate and availability of private sector finance are outside of their control.

Reputation risk

- dependent on a good reputation in order to generate future revenue.

- link reputational effect with competitive nature of the market

- problems with project overruns or poor build quality leading to loss of future business

- publicity given to such problems would also potentially lose revenue with future clients.

- problems on site may not be within Bild's control.

Staffing risk

- dependent on the recruitment and retention of good quality, highly motivated staff

- link to reputation risk, problems with staff motivation could lead to build quality issues

- significant proportion of Bild's revenue comes from repeat business and retaining key staff that have a good relationship with clients will be important for revenue generation.

Financial facilities

- future revenue dependent on sufficient financial facilities; clients pay in stages not in advance

- Bild Development contributes to revenue and profit but requires significant cash investment.

- accurate cash flow forecasting is therefore necessary but may be difficult due to the complexity of the business and the level of uncertainty caused by issues outside Bild's control (e.g. weather, construction start dates, development sale dates)

Part (b)

Challenges associated with developing and implementing a management strategy

Hiring and retaining the right people

- a major challenge for the board, given the cyclical nature of the construction industry

- e.g. market is buoyant, there will be a shortage of skilled workers and managers;

- e.g. market in decline, decisions regarding which staff to retain, and which to make redundant.

Strategic planning

- a challenging and evolving market, for example PPP opportunities may now be available to Bild.

- constant need to examine trends and innovations

- how to differentiate themselves from competitors

- how client behaviours are changing

Succession planning

- need to develop future managers with leadership and business skills.

- e.g. project managers need to understand the financial impact of their actions on cash flows

- developing and promoting the best managers will help build a culture of long term client relationships.

Organisational structure

- a complex organisation.

- offices are located throughout Ceeland, projects vary from small units to very large

- management skills needed for civil engineering, development and investment are different.

- need to build a sustainable organisation to minimise dysfunctional decision making.

Note: The key lesson to learn here is that the answer consists of the application of relevant points made to BILD.

5 Exam Task 2

Review of marking guide

The part of the marking guide that relates to this task is as follows:

Section	Technical skills	Business Skills	People Skills		Leadership Skills		Integration	Total
2			Communication	8	Motivation	15	2	25

It is always worth reviewing marking guides to check that you are happy with the total marks and how different tasks relate to the competences.

- This section again had a time allocation of 45 minutes, so was worth 25% of the marks

- Advise on clear and effective communication amongst the board members – people skills

- Motivate and encourage collaboration between executive and non-executive directors – leadership skills

Examiner's comments

The examiner's specific comments on task 2 were as follows:

"This question deals with the relationship between the executive and non-executive directors. Both parts of the question require some thought about the implications of having this distinction. Arguably, the non-executives have a supervisory role that could put them at odds with the executive colleagues. Answers should address that potential for antagonism."

Understanding the model answer

The first part of the task requires you to consider how to ensure clear and effective communication between the different categories of board members which allows you to address the syllabus area of the effectiveness of organisational relationships. To this extent the effectiveness of the communication between the executive and non-executive directors is the responsibility of the Chairman as this will ensure the effectiveness if the board. It is important that you address this responsibility as soon as possible in your answer and then relate you answer to the pre-seen information and best practices otherwise the response will be merely a list of recognised effective communication tools.

The second part of the task asks you how to motivate the executive directors to make the best possible use of the contribution that the non-executives directors can provide. In this context, it will be important for the executive directors to understand their role and how the expertise they offer can provide significant advantages.

The fact that you are asked "How" indicates that your answer should contain some recommended approaches to resolving the issue e.g. based on the success of the work with the non-executives outlined in task 1, extending this to incorporate the executive directors also.

The third part of the task required a consideration of how to manage the changing roles of both categories of directors. The suggested solution has incorporated the response to the second and third part of the requirement and to some extent this makes perfect sense given that the approach suggested for the second part also fits well with the third part.

Given this we can see that the model answer is structured as follows:

Part (a)

How can we ensure clear and effective communication between the executive and the non-executive directors?

- identify responsibility – part of the role of the chairman.

- the appointment of a strong chair, and making this part of his job description, is important.

- an induction program for executive and non-executive directors alike to ensure what time commitment they are expected to give.

- ensuring the right people are appointed as non-executive directors who have useful experience, communication should be straightforward.

- having diversity on the Board with the right mix of skills and experience will facilitate good communication.

- all directors are given adequate information in a timely manner and of good quality.

- part of the Chairman's role to ensure an agenda and information are communicated to the executive and non-executive directors.

- information should be clear to all directors whatever their skills and expertise. The board needs information analysed in an insightful manner if it is to communicate effectively

- e.g. Finance Director's duty is to ensure that the financial information presented to the board is understandable to directors who do not have an accounting qualification.

- this would apply to all discussions in any discipline: marketing, strategy, HR etc.

Part (b)

How can we motivate the executive directors to make best use of the non-executive contribution? How can we manage the changing roles of the executive and non-executive directors?

- danger that executive directors do not understand the role non-executives and may see no genuine benefit from the presence of non-execs.

- the training exercise for non-executives was a success carry out similar training for executive directors to better understand the role and benefits of the non-execs.

- training carried out regularly, perhaps annually, to ensure that directors are aware of the changing roles.

- an induction package should be an essential part of the introduction of all new directors to the company.

- should discuss many of the duties that the directors will be expected to perform, introduce them to all the people they will be working with and answer any questions the new director has.

- in order to motivate the exec directors it may also be necessary for them to see for themselves the benefit of the non-execs. Telling them that there are benefits may not be enough.

- improvements in communication set out above should assist – if the directors are communicating effectively the benefits of the non-execs should be readily apparent.

- the non-execs must have credibility with the exec directors recruitment of individuals with appropriate experience, good business judgement and integrity is vital.

- responsibility of the non-execs here, to challenge the executive board and present alternative to those held by the other board members.

- importance of tact and diplomacy for a non-exec.

- the role of the chairman is important who has responsibility to ensure meetings are effective.

6 Exam Task 3

Review of marking guide

The part of the marking guide that relates to this task is as follows:

Section	Technical skills		Business Skills	People Skills		Leadership Skills	Integration	Total
3	Control of hiring	14		Negotiation of transfer prices	10		1	25

It is always worth reviewing marking guides to check that you are happy with the total marks and how different tasks relate to the competences.

- This section again had a time allocation of 45 minutes, so was worth 25% of the marks

- Provide advice on the difficulties associated with the two transfer pricing options. You may have been surprised to see that these difficulties were considered people skills rather than technical.

- Which option will reduce dysfunctional behaviour and explain how this will resolve any conflicts – technical skills

Examiner's comments

The examiner's specific comments on task 3 were as follows:

"The first part of the question deals with the difficulties associated with avoiding dysfunctional behaviour associated with transfer pricing, when third parties sometimes offer keener prices than can be obtained from an internal transfer of a resource that is surplus and so would have no net cost to the entity as a whole.

The second part of the question looks at the same problem in terms of establishing controls to prevent the occurrence of such dysfunctional behaviour. This requires some understanding of the mechanics of selecting suppliers and initiating transactions". In this context therefore there would be a need to refer to how to control these transactions.

Understanding the model answer

The first part of the task requires you to consider the difficulties associated with the options available to control transfer pricing. This means that you need to apply your knowledge of the principles of transfer pricing to the circumstances facing BILD. In this context you need to draw on the information from both the pre-seen and trigger email, in particular the attractive prices for equipment from outside third parties.

The second part then requires you to select the best option to reduce the dysfunctional behaviour of hiring equipment from the external third parties and then explain how it will resolve any conflicts. It may surprise you to learn that this requirement draws on your knowledge if internal control and in that respect, carries technical marks from the syllabus for P2 i.e. – discuss issues arising from the use of performance measures and budgets for control.

The model answer is structured as follows:

Part (a) What are the difficulties associated with the two options?

- set transfer prices below the prices charged by third parties it is unlikely to be sufficient to solve the problem, despite encouraging internal discussion

- note that equipment hire prices are likely to fluctuate and vary widely from location to location

- it would therefore be necessary to either re-set transfer prices frequently, to undercut any hire quote received outside the Bild group

- this process of obtaining an external hire quotation, and then asking for an internal bid against it, could be too cumbersome.

- set transfer prices very low, to just cover any incremental costs incurred by the lender encouraging managers to borrow internally, might make them less willing to lend.

- to encourage divisional managers to borrow equipment in house make this measure part of a balanced scorecard appraisal.

- alternatively set up an internal database detailing surplus equipment is held at each location, making it a straightforward exercise for managers to find what they need.

Part (b) which option will reduce the dysfunctional behaviour; how will this help to resolve any conflicts?

- Bild will tend to hire large items of plant for prolonged periods, therefore the cost of each hire contract will be substantial and worth investing time and effort in its control.

- establish a plant hire department that authorises all hire contracts costing more than a pre-set limit, staffed by people with some understanding of the role of each item of equipment being hired.

- the department should be responsible for placing any orders for hire so that the regional subsidiaries do not simply hire from third parties as a matter of course

- all requests to be accompanied by full supporting information for the hire

- asset register should be checked first before hire considered

- register should show location of the equipment and whether it is available for use (NB these would be further fields that would not normally be found on a typical asset register).

- in deciding whether to use an asset belonging to a fellow division, the plant hire department should take account of the cost of transporting the asset to and from the site.

- the plant hire department should estimate the cost of hiring the equipment commercially and should process an internal charge that is based on this market price to ensure hirer is not paying any more than would have been charged by a third party.

- department should also be analysing external hires to determine any assets that should be bought outright rather than hiring them

- a central record of hires will identify items of equipment are hired so frequently that it would be cheaper to buy them instead

7 Exam Task 4

Review of marking guide

The part of the marking guide that relates to this task is as follows:

Section	Technical skills		Business Skills	People Skills	Leadership Skills	Integration	Total
4	Tax, pricing	12	Reput-ation	12		1	25

It is always worth reviewing marking guides to check that you are happy with the total marks and how different tasks relate to the competences.

- This section again had a time allocation of 45 minutes, so was worth 25% of the marks

- Provide advice on the potential effectiveness of a new tax arrangement to reduce tax expense of BILD. This advice is to be provided from a tax management point of view – technical skills.

- What would be the impact of the arrangement on BILD's market environment – business skills?

Examiner's comments

The examiner's specific comments on task 4 were as follows:

"This question deals with the very topical issue of using artificial transfers to manage the overall tax liability.

The first part of the question is looking for an understanding of how such an arrangement may or may not prove successful. In practice, it may be difficult to persuade the tax authorities to accept that an artificial scheme should stand.

The second part of the question is looking at the broader implications. It has been established that there can be reputational issues associated with such schemes. Any building company will be keen to win major government contracts, which may be more difficult to obtain if the company has a reputation for tax avoidance".

Understanding the model answer

The first part of the task requires you to consider the effectiveness of the newly proposed tax arrangement. That is to say will it work and will its application be legitimately accepted by the tax authorities. This means that you need to apply your knowledge of tax avoidance schemes and the parameters under which their proposals may be accepted in the light of the circumstances facing BILD. In this context you need to draw on the information from both the pre-seen and trigger email and, in addition, it would be beneficial to draw upon the highly publicised real world examples of such schemes.

The second part then requires you to consider the wider aspects of the application of such a scheme to the credibility of BILD as a provider of building services in the highly competitive construction industry and the impact that this may have on the firm's competitive advantage.

The model answer is structured as follows:

Part (a)

- consider the variability of global tax rates vary globally

- consider the rate currently paid by BILD in Ceeland's rate of 35% which is high

- consider the existence of schemes exist where international companies seek to establish subsidiaries in the most advantageous tax locations.

- real world example would be useful here and demonstrate appropriate and relevant industry research e.g. example Starbucks or Fiat.

- consider BILD's corporate status and geography of its activities and draw comparisons with the above examples

- consider what would make the scheme successful and develop the link with transfer pricing e.g. BILD procurement would have to buy construction materials at market prices and then sell them on to BILD at an inflated transfer price, leading to profits in BILD Procurement's low tax jurisdiction country.

- consider Ceeland tax authorities challenge to the arrangement unless BILD can prove the price paid to BILD Procurement is a fair market price as construction materials prices are easily established

- BILD Procurement could probably justify an administration charge on top of market price; this is not going to be sufficient to shift profits to a lower tax jurisdiction

- consider the fact that BILD will pay prices set in $, and not have a physical office, or staff based overseas

- impossible to argue that this is not an artificial transaction designed purely to avoid tax.

Conclude – This scheme is unlikely to be successful.

Part (b)

General comment:

Bild is under pressure to cut costs in order to remain competitive. Tax paid is one of those costs. Reducing the effective tax rate should, in theory, make BILD more competitive.

- consider the danger of reputational damage from this move.

- Consider reaction from BILD's client base, i.e. some clients may wish to source construction as cheaply as possible and not be interested in the tax arrangements of the builder

- consider business with the public sector in Ceeland and new PPP opportunities with the Ceeland Government

- likelihood that the government would be willing to enter into a partnership with a company which is deliberately setting out to exploit tax loopholes

- examples of other companies have suffered reputational damage and loss of revenue when such arrangements have been made public – in the UK, Starbucks and Amazon

- consider the competitive reaction to a reputational breach; competitors would act to ensure that it was well-publicised.

- the attempt to reduce tax in this way would have a repercussive effect on BILD; a failed tax avoidance scheme (with associated costs) and negative publicity.

8 Integration marks

There are 9 integration marks available in this variant paper with marks spread across each of the tasks. These marks will be awarded for the overall quality of your answer and use of available information. You should consider the style and language you use and ensure it is suitable for the intended recipient. It is also important that your responses are appropriately structured and logical.